PARIS

JEREMY BLACK

PARIS

A Short History

For Patrick Manning

Frontispiece: The Arc de Triomphe.

First published in the United Kingdom in 2024 by
Thames & Hudson Ltd, 181A High Holborn, London WC1V 7QX

First published in the United States of America in 2024 by
Thames & Hudson Inc., 500 Fifth Avenue, New York, New York 10110

Paris: A Short History © 2024 Thames & Hudson Ltd, London
Text © 2024 Jeremy Black

Designed by Sam Clark

British Library Cataloguing-in-Publication Data
A catalogue record for this book is available from the British Library

Library of Congress Control Number 2023944866

ISBN 978-0-500-02708-0

Printed and bound in China by Toppan Leefung Printing Limited

MIX
Paper from
responsible sources
FSC® C104723
FSC
www.fsc.org

Be the first to know about our new releases,
exclusive content and author events by visiting
thamesandhudson.com
thamesandhudsonusa.com
thamesandhudson.com.au

TABLE OF CONTENTS

Introduction

The Inevitability of Paris

'*That metropolis of dress and debauchery*'
—Scottish poet David Mallet, describing Paris in 1735

Paris, a city with a known history of more than two millennia, is arguably more significant today than ever before. Its status as a place of global consequence – the capital of a major empire, and a leading light in a Europe that spanned the globe with its influence – is relatively recent. Yet there is no simple way of measuring a city's importance. It may be intellectually formidable, as Paris was in the eighteenth century when it was the centre of the Western Enlightenment, or culturally vibrant, as it was in the 1890s and again in the 1920s, without necessarily being at some political apex.

The relationship between Paris and the rest of France is complex and varied. As a capital it has long been not only a centre of power but a source of new initiatives and demands, many of them deeply unpopular elsewhere in the country – a situation that continues to this day. In his 1830 novel *Scarlet and Black*, Stendhal presents the Church as opposed to the role and example of Paris, with one cleric remarking that it is no longer Napoleon who is the problem: 'Today, it is not a man that we must destroy – it is Paris. The whole of France copies Paris. What is the use of arming your five hundred men in each Department…in a matter which is peculiar to Paris?

Paris alone, with her newspapers and her drawing-rooms, has done the damage; let this modern Babylon perish.'

The history of Paris, then, is the history of a city, a culture, a society and a state. It cannot be separated from the history of France. But there is also an excitement peculiar to the city, one that rings round the clock. Capturing this vibrant quality requires a focus on recent centuries, and in particular on the way in which Paris as we see it now has been constructed and experienced.

Paris has long been celebrated as a place of style, wit and sensuality; it is, among other things, a showcase for art and culture, and life there is an art in itself. Its intoxicating character was captured in the seventeenth century by Madame de Sévigné's remark, 'One does not get over Paris.' Ever since that period, as international tourism blossomed, visitors from all over the world have been variously fascinated, delighted and intimidated by the city. In Émile Zola's *La Bête humaine* (1890), twenty-five-year-old Séverine Aubry is up from Le Havre: 'Coming to Paris always went to her head. She was all excited with the joy of being foot-loose on the pavements, and was still thrilled with her purchases at the Bon Marché.' Her husband, however, worries about these absences: 'He never had any suspicions at Le Havre, but in Paris he thought of all kinds of dangers, deceptions and misdeeds.' There are the 'giddy horizons of Paris' of Colette's sensual *La Chatte* (1933).

Today, the tourist repertoire can be very fixed, but there are many places that deserve more attention than they habitually receive. This is particularly true of the city's outlying areas and of buildings constructed between 1850 and 1960, including churches, railway stations and those of unfamiliar design or material – for instance, the Église Saint-Jean-de-Montmartre, the first church in Paris to be built of reinforced concrete. From the same period, near the Place de Catalogne in south-west Paris, comes the Église

Notre-Dame-du-Travail with its bare iron girders, designed to appeal to the working-class parishioners of this poor area. Built between 1899 and 1902 according to the design of Jules Astruc, who was inspired in part by the Eiffel Tower, the church was intended to honour workers and bring them to God. Its Romanesque sandstone façade gives the passer-by no hint of the distinctive and spacious interior, which incorporates 135 tonnes of iron and steel.

Nearby in the 14th arrondissement is the Jardin des Colonnes, another of the city's lesser-known and unexpected pleasures: a small park encircled by a neoclassical building with a striking expanse of mirrored windows, designed in 1986 by the Catalan architect Ricardo Bofill. And in the 15th is the Jardin Atlantique, a public park opened in 1994 – tucked away among ugly modern office buildings, it incorporates thoughtfully designed thematic gardens laid out across the roof of the Gare Montparnasse.

One way of deciding on a path into the history of Paris is to follow the work of a particular artist or architect. This approach can lead the tourist far afield: to follow Le Corbusier means exploring not only his well-known works in Auteuil, but also the Brazilian and Swiss halls of the Cité Internationale Universitaire. I spent a week there in 1980, in the American hall, while carrying out archival research in central Paris. It's a fair bet that the 100-acre complex is known by very few tourists, but it includes a number of interesting interwar and postwar buildings – in effect, it is an architectural park. Easy to reach by RER train to the Cité Universitaire stop, it pairs well with a visit to the Parc Montsouris, which offers a contrasting landscape in the 1870s English style.

It is also worth remembering that a fresh look at the familiar can shed new light on the city's history. Two of the great Paris museums have recently been modernized with the addition of brand-new spaces, exhibits and visitor resources: the Museum of the History of Paris in the Hôtel Carnavalet, and the Cluny Museum of medieval art.

Buildings and museums aside, there are plenty of less traditional ways to engage with the history of Paris and trace its political, social, economic and cultural narratives. The political is perhaps the most significant – after all, it was politics that made Paris the capital of France and thus a centre of struggle as its destiny was contested. It was Paris that the English attempted to control in the Hundred Years' War, the Catholic League in the Wars of Religion, the Revolutionaries in the Revolution, the Allies in 1814 and 1815, the Germans in 1870–1, 1914 and 1940, and de Gaulle in 1944. Revolution has centred on this city more than on any other French city. Paris's political significance has served as a magnet for power, wealth and influence, and it has accordingly set the scene for all of these. Lyon might offer food, Bordeaux wine, Marseille the sun on the Mediterranean – but Paris is the stage and centre for all.

Chapter I

Early Days

The Arènes de Lutèce is not, as its name might suggest, a modern football stadium, but a Roman arena tucked away in Paris's 5th arrondissement, where it lay buried for centuries before being rediscovered in 1869 during Baron Haussmann's street-building conquest of the city. Constructed in the second century CE and destroyed in the late third by 'barbarian' attackers, it is a strikingly theatrical space that would have hosted the many and varied public displays of ancient Roman culture. Today, however, far more attention tends to be paid to Paris as a later stage for more ancient works, from the Luxor Obelisk in the Place de la Concorde to the Winged Victory of Samothrace in the Louvre.

Paris, even more so than London, has a pre-Roman history and was a place of consequence in the ancient world. The Musée Carnavalet, the museum of the history of Paris, holds Neolithic finds discovered in the 1990s including wooden canoes from the Bercy area. Yet it is as a result of Roman conquest that Paris first appears in written history, its name given by Julius Caesar as 'Lutetia' when he summoned a meeting of conquered Gauls there in 53 BCE.

Lutetia – capital of the Parisii, a relatively modest Gallic tribe – was at that time confined to the Île de la Cité, the largest island in the river Seine, which they had settled from about 200 BCE. An island site gave the tribe protection from raiders as well as plenty of opportunity to profit from trade along the river, which has always been a central part of the history of Paris. At 777 kilometres long (nearly 500 miles), the Seine rises north-west of Dijon and reaches the Channel at Le Havre. Most of its length is readily navigable and it has numerous tributaries, including the Aube, Eure, Loing, Marne, Oise and Yonne, that greatly extend its influence.

In particular, the Seine represented a means of shipping goods that were not widely obtainable, had to be brought in, and therefore had particular value, notably tin (essential in the Bronze Age for the production of bronze), iron and salt. It offered fishing as well. Moreover, although the island made the river faster – thus increasing its defensive capacity – it also served as a stepping stone that made crossing easier, boosting its importance for trade.

In 52 BCE Caesar's deputy, Titus Labienus, defeated the Parisii in the Battle of Lutetia. Now that the city was securely Roman, it rapidly grew in significance. The remains of the ancient public baths, dating from about 200 CE, are an impressive part of the Musée de Cluny (named for the Abbot of Cluny, who purchased the ruins in 1330). What survives of them represents about a third of the extent of the original complex. They are now below ground level, which diminishes their grandeur and serves to remind today's visitors of how much more of Lutetia has been obliterated by subsequent building. This is also more generally true of Paris, which is multi-layered in many respects. Architecturally, the layering is particularly characteristic of the historic city centre, but it can also be seen in former ancillary settlements and buildings such as churches as well as outlying roads and bridges. There were once

Roman roads radiating out from the location of modern-day Paris in a number of directions: down the Seine to Harfleur, to Évreux further west, and south-east to Sens and Troyes.

The cold-water bath, the frigidarium, is the most impressive remaining part of the public baths, but a steam room, a warm-water bath and a gymnasium all survive. So does the 'Pilier des nautes' or Boatmen's Pillar, a monument dedicated to Jupiter by the guild of boatmen (merchants who used the Seine) in the early first century CE and subsequently rediscovered on the Île de la Cité, having been reused in the city wall (see plate 1).

An archaeological crypt beneath the square in front of Notre-Dame Cathedral provides a view of Lutetia's buildings and streets, as well as part of the third-century wall. It also has good scale models of the development of the city. In the nineteenth century it was wrongly assumed that the baths had been the Imperial Palace, where Julian the Apostate was proclaimed Roman emperor in 360. Traces of the Roman wall can also be seen in the Rue de la Colombe, Île de la Cité.

While the island was Lutetia's centre, another important site on the river's left bank provided valuable space for expansion. This bank was higher than the right, making it less prone to flooding and therefore better for construction – reducing the risk of damp, with its misery and unhealthiness, and of waterlogged cellars that would compromise storage at or below ground level. The Left Bank developed into a city centre comparable to London's, but the latter lacked any equivalent to the Cité. At the same time, the added security provided by the Cité was a possible challenge to the future of the Left Bank.

There were more prominent and powerful cities in Roman France (or Gaul, as it was known) – notably Lugdunum (Lyon), the political capital and, until the third century, the commercial

PARIS
SOUS LES ROMAINS
Échelle de 1/160.000
Kilomètres
0   1/2   1   2

Hauteurs de Challlot
et de Passy

Voie d' Issy

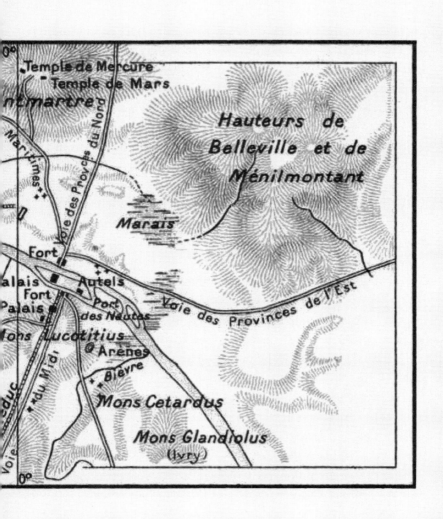

Temple de Mercure
Temple de Mars
ntmartre
Maritimes
Voie des Provinces du Nord
Marais
Hauteurs de
Belleville et de
Ménilmontant
Fort
alais
Autels
Fort
Palais
Port
des Nautes
Voie des Provinces de l'Est
ons Lucotitius
Arènes
Bièvre
Mons Cetardus
Mons Glandiolus
(Ivry)
Voie du Midi
Voie
duc
0°
0°

centre. Paris nevertheless acquired buildings equivalent to those that characterized Roman cities in the Mediterranean, and was linked to its surroundings by roads and bridges. The roads to the south-east connected Paris to Lyon and thence to Italy, with a particularly important route from Lyon down the Rhône.

An increase in attacks on Roman Paris during the late third and fourth centuries prompted improvements in fortification. It was towards the end of the third century, a period of rebellion and invasion, that one such attack destroyed the baths. At around this time many elite residents relocated to rural villas, where they enjoyed a degree of self-reliance. This, however, undermined the city's status, reducing its revenues and eventually its significance.

Meanwhile, another major cultural shift was occurring as Christianity replaced the imperial pantheon of gods. There was martyrdom along the way: Saint Denis, first bishop of Paris, was allegedly beheaded on the hill of Montmartre around 250, during the persecution of Christians carried out by the emperor Decius (r. 249–51). It was said that he picked up his decapitated head and walked for some distance, preaching as he went. Later, the martyrdom of the twin saints Gervase and Protase led to the foundation of the sixth-century church of Saint-Gervais-Saint-Protais, which has since been rebuilt and is situated on the right bank of the Seine, east of the Hôtel de Ville (City Hall).

Governmental significance was suggested by the town becoming a residence of Constantius Chlorus, one of four co-emperors from 293 to 305. He ruled Roman Britain, France, Germany up to the Rhine, and the Low Countries. Trier on the Moselle was his capital, and has more imposing remains than Paris; nevertheless, the latter was a residence of this much-travelled commander. As another sign of political and military significance, Julian the Apostate was proclaimed emperor and raised aloft on a shield here in 360 by his troops; it was the third year in which he had wintered in the city while campaigning against the Alamanni on the Rhine frontier. Lutetia made an appropriate headquarters while he drove them back across the river. The same year, the city was renamed Paris – but Julian made Constantinople, of which he gained control in 361, his capital.

Julian was killed in 363 by the Sasanians at the Battle of Samarra in Mesopotamia. He was succeeded by his cousin Jovian, who in turn died – possibly poisoned – in 364 and was succeeded by Valentinian I (r. 365–75) as ruler of the empire's western provinces. A fresh invasion of Gaul by the Alamanni in 365 led Valentinian to focus on the region and he spent time in Paris, finally defeating the invaders. His eldest son, Gratian (r. 367–83), a co-ruler in the late Roman pattern, succeeded in the western dominions and also spent some time in Paris, although his capitals were Trier and Milan.

Paris was the site of a decisive confrontation in 383 between Gratian and Magnus Maximus, commander of the Roman forces in Britain who had rebelled and invaded Gaul. Gratian's army was largely defeated and he fled, to be killed at Lyon; Maximus then made his capital at Trier. His vanquisher, Theodosius I, made his capital in Milan, while his successor in the west used Milan and then Ravenna. The Goths' challenge to Italy – and therefore Rome – from the Danube frontier made the Rhine and Gaul frontiers militarily peripheral and led to them losing defenders, opening the way to invasions. The Goths would take full advantage of this, eventually leading to the fall of Gaul.

Chapter 2

―

Early Medieval Paris

For a visitor interested in early medieval Paris, the most important place to see is not in the centre of the city but in a suburb several kilometres to the north: Saint-Denis, which was formerly located beyond the city walls.

Saint-Denis originated as a Roman settlement, Catolacus, located on the road heading north from Paris – a key route at the time. A site of religious significance owing to its association with the eponymous martyr, it eventually became the wealthiest French abbey. Several distinct stages of building took place there – in the 470s, early seventh century, 750s, 1130s–40s, and thirteenth century – resulting in an amalgam of styles in which the latter stages are most important.

The ambitious Abbot Suger (*c.* 1081–1151), an influential royal adviser who was part of the chain of connection between Crown and Church that would be so important to the development of the capital, played a key role in the rebuilding of the church during the 1130s and 1140s, when it became a masterpiece of Gothic style. The basilica was extensively restored in the late nineteenth century but a sense of the medieval mind may still be gathered by contemplating the carvings above its central doorway, which depict not only the Last Judgment but also the last communion of the saint and his martyrdom.

A visit to Saint-Denis reminds us that there is much more to Paris than its well-known tourist centre – a point that many visitors tend to forget, even if they make the obligatory trip to Versailles. While it is more compact than London or Tokyo, Paris is still extensive, and its history incorporates a number of important sites that were once outside its walls.

Saint-Denis represents one legacy of Rome, in the shape of Christianity, but the empire had gone by the time it became established. Instead, the fifth century saw the conquest of Gaul by 'barbarian' invaders. This, however, did not lead to the destruction of Paris; as the story goes, the threat of devastation by Attila the Hun in 451 was deflected from the city by Saint Geneviève, who won heavenly support through the organization of mass prayer. In 464, moreover, she brought food to the island-city when it was besieged by the Frankish leader Childeric I, father of Clovis I. Geneviève became patroness saint of Paris and is celebrated across the city, particularly in paintings within the Panthéon, which was originally a church dedicated to her (see plate x). There is also Michel-Louis Victor Mercier's 1845 statue beside the pond in the Luxembourg Gardens, and a striking statue by Paul Landowski on the Pont de la Tournelle, which has a dramatic view of Notre-Dame's east end.

The Franks, whose name meant 'free' or 'fierce ones', had by this time become the dominant group across much of northern France and Belgium; all the more so following the victory at Soissons in 486 by Clovis, their king (r. 481–c. 511), over the surviving Romano-Gaullish army. Legitimation and the support of the Gallo-Roman aristocracy came from Clovis converting to Christianity, which encouraged a bridging of cultures. He was baptized at Reims,

80 miles (129 kilometres) north-east of Paris, probably in 496 – a step that led Geneviève to persuade Paris to accept his authority. Paris became his capital in 508. It provided an echo of imperial government and power under Rome, and was controlled by him as other such centres were not. He would become known as the founder of the Merovingian dynasty, rulers of much of what became France. Indeed, the Merovingians can be regarded as the first kings of France.

The old Roman administrative buildings on the Île de la Cité were used by the new ruler. They had the virtue of being built in stone and were therefore fireproof, a highly valued quality at a time when open flames were routinely used in heating and lighting. Stone offered security as well as longevity. It was more difficult to replace than wood, which encouraged its re-use for other purposes or, in the case of palaces, churches and fortresses, adaptation into new structures.

Geneviève herself was buried, like Clovis, in the church of the Abbey of Saint Geneviève, which added to the city's status. The same site is now occupied by the Panthéon, a building dating to the 1750s that was originally conceived by Louis XV (see plate VIII) as an imposing church in her honour. In the porch of the Church of Saint-Germain-l'Auxerrois, a much later work, she is shown holding a candle that a devil is seeking to snuff out.

Paris was a Roman city, which helped to provide legitimacy as well as shelter, especially when Clovis agreed to rule as a form of honorary consul on behalf of the Byzantine (Eastern Roman) Emperor. Furthermore, like Reims, Paris was a Christian centre. The Cathedral of Saint-Étienne was built in the fourth, fifth or sixth century to the west of where Notre-Dame would later stand. It probably stood on the site of an earlier Roman temple dating to the fifth century (and rebuilt in the sixth). The cathedral was about 70 metres (230 feet) long, with four aisles as well as the nave;

LUTECE
ou
PREMIER PLAN
DE LA VILLE DE PARIS
Tiré
De Cesar, de Strabon, de l'Empereur
Julien, et d'Ammian Marcellin.
Par
M. L. C. D. L. M.
1705.

SEINE R.

Bois.

Bois.

Bois.

Bois.

Bou.

Temple d'Isis
ou de Ceres.

Prez.

Prez.

DESCRIPTION

Cette petite Ville que les Gaulois nommoient LUTECE étoit la
Capitale de la Province des Parisiens, l'une des 64. qui com-
posoient tout l'Etat des Gaules.
Elle étoit renfermée dans l'une des Isles de la Seine, le côté
du Nord couvert d'un Marais et d'un Bois, et celuy du Midy
une partie en Prez, et le reste aussi en Marais et
en Bois.
Ses Maisons étoient de forme ronde bâtie de Bois et de
Terre couvertes de Roseaux ou de Pailles et sans Chemi-
nées.
Camulogene en étoit le Gouverneur ou Souverain
Magistrat lorsque les Romains en firent la conquête
l'an du Monde 3998. et avant N. S. I. C. 56. ans.

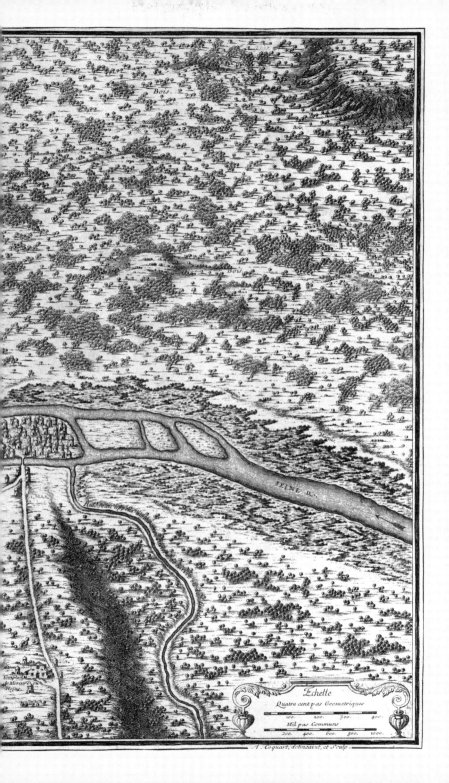

Bois.

Bois.

Bois.

SEINE. R.

Ruisseau appellé

Temple
de Mercure, ou
Helio.

Echelle
Quatre cent pas Geometriques
100. 200. 300. 400.
Mil par Commune
200. 400. 600. 800. 1000.

A. Coquart, delineavit, et Sculp.

it was demolished when Notre-Dame was built. There was also a chapel established by Saint Geneviève in 475 on the site where Saint Denis died; this was where the Basilica of Saint-Denis now stands, and the first king to be buried there was Dagobert I, who died in 639. The church's role as a funeral marker for the dynasty, a mausoleum of note, was evident during a 1959 archaeological excavation of the crypt that revealed the late sixth-century tomb of Aregund (*c.* 515–80), one of the wives of Chlothar I, complete with clothing and jewelry.

There were other churches in the Paris area, too; their frequency was a sign of the city's importance and also helped to reinforce it. Completed in 558, the Church of Saint-Germain-des-Prés was founded to house a relic of Saint Vincent. The Church of Saint-Pierre de Montmartre, allegedly founded by Saint Denis, can be more accurately dated to the sixth century and was probably based originally on a Roman temple of Mars, which may have been the source of the district's name. It may have been developed in the ninth century into a chapel of martyrs in honour of Saint Denis, serving as a stop for pilgrims en route to his basilica. In 1133, Louis VI founded a convent in Montmartre and the church is now all that remains.

On the standard Frankish pattern, Clovis's kingdom was partitioned by his four sons and then, after being reunited by one of these (Chlothar I), partitioned anew on his death in 561. One of the key units – Neustria, in the north-west of the Frankish area – had a capital at Paris. Neustria competed with the other units, Austrasia, Burgundy and Aquitania, but Paris also competed as capital even of its 'near area' with Orléans, Reims and Soissons. Indeed, early Church councils of the Frankish Church began in Orléans in 511 rather than Paris. Paris was simply a bishopric, with Sens as its archdiocese; and life there could be highly precarious, with wolves and bears living in the ancient oak forest now known as the Bois de Boulogne.

Neustria defended the unity of the Frankish kingdom and was threatened by attack from Germanic tribes to the east or Moors to the south. Nevertheless, Paris was not the key city even when the Merovingian dynasty of Frankish rulers was replaced by the Carolingians. Pépin the Short (r. 751–68), the first Carolingian king, had been educated at Saint-Denis, where (having previously been anointed in 751, in Soissons) he was anointed in 754 by Pope Stephen II – the first crowning of a civil ruler by a pope. He and his wife are buried at Saint-Denis.

The empire-making Charlemagne (r. 768–814), crowned at Noyon in 768 and by the Pope as emperor in Rome in 800, spent little time in Paris; instead he spent most of his life on campaign, notably against the Saxons. He established his capital at Aachen, which became a ceremonial centre for the dynasty and where he called a Church council. It was there that he died and was buried. In turn, Paris became the capital of the kingdom of West Francia (roughly coterminous with modern France), created when Charlemagne's empire was divided among his heirs in 817 and 843 – although the association of the western branch of the Carolingians with the city was limited.

Paris was unsuccessfully besieged by the Vikings in 885–6, an important episode of the city's history that underlined the defensive value of the Île de la Cité and the contrasting vulnerability of the suburbs on the other banks of the Seine. The monastery of Saint-Germain-des-Prés was largely destroyed, and would not be rebuilt until about 1000. Vikings had attacked Paris with success on several previous occasions from 845 onwards, but the siege of 885–6 was the largest operation yet. Despite being outnumbered, Odo, Count of Paris provided an effective defence, making use of fortified bridges to block passage up the river. The prestige gained by his victory helped in the rise of the Capetian dynasty.

Odo's defence of Paris was celebrated in various historical paintings of the nineteenth century; for example, Jean-Victor Schnetz's *Count Odo defends Paris against the Norsemen* (1837), which, commissioned by Louis Philippe in 1834, hangs in the Galerie des Batailles in Versailles – as does Ary Scheffer's *Battle of Tolbiac*, which recalled Clovis I's victory over the Alamanni in 496. Scheffer was another protégé of Louis Philippe, and his home in Montmartre is now the Musée de la Vie Romantique, exhibiting his own work alongside that of other Romantic figures.

Paris was also adopted as the capital by the Capetian successors to the Carolingians. The Capetians had a strong link with Paris; Count Odo's father, Robert the Strong (c. 830–866), had established the family in Neustria. After Odo had resisted the Viking siege of Paris he became king of West Francia, and his brother Robert eventually succeeded him in both roles. Robert's grandson was the Paris-born Hugh Capet, who became king of the Franks in 987, being elected at Noyon and crowned in Reims. He was elected against the claim to the crown of the legitimate Carolingian, Charles of Lorraine, because unlike the latter Capet was a French noble with French, rather than German, as his native tongue.

The Capetians had scant power but nevertheless retained the kingship for 300 years while Paris's position as capital developed under Hugh's son, Robert II the Pious (r. 996–1031), who focused on the city, developing the royal presence on the Île de la Cité. In 1007, the County of Paris reverted to the Crown from the family of the counts of Vendôme. Royal power over the archdiocese of Sens was increased, which affected the situation in Paris. Robert's son, Henry I (r. 1031–60), faced serious problems with his major vassals – in effect other French rulers, notably Duke William of Normandy. The Vikings had by now established themselves in Normandy, which was ceded to them as a duchy in 911. William's conquest of England in 1066 made Normandy a major power and therefore a significant threat to the Capetians.

Henry rebuilt the Priory of Saint-Martin-des-Champs, which dated from the early eighth century but had been destroyed by Normans (Vikings) in the late tenth century. His son, Philip I (r. 1060–1108), later presented the priory to the Abbey of Cluny. Like his father, Philip faced various battles with his vassals, and he had poor relations with Saint-Denis. In contrast, his son Louis VI (r. 1108–37) was close to the abbey and particularly to its abbot, the aforementioned Suger, who wrote his biography. Louis worked to suppress robber barons in the area around Paris as well as fighting troublesome vassals including Henry I of England, then Duke of Normandy. In 1124, in response to a threat of invasion by the emperor Henry V, the dominant figure in Germany, Louis presented himself as the vassal of Saint Denis and began carrying his banner in a bid for support and unity among the barons; the invasion never took place.

Louis's son, Louis VII (r. 1137–80), continued to favour Abbot Suger, who served as one of the regents during the king's absence on the Second Crusade. Meanwhile, Henry, Duke of Normandy, who was Count of Anjou and, from 1154, Henry II of England, became an even greater threat by marrying Eleanor of Aquitaine, heiress of much of south-west France.

The role of Saint-Denis, as of Saint-Remi at Reims, continued to be significant; these sacred sites were of great importance to the holiness of the king's person. Ancestors and epic leaders of the past were depicted on tomb effigies in the choirs of both basilicas.

The Crown controlled the Archbishopric of Sens, with the right of nomination to it, as to Reims, and also to a number of bishoprics including Paris. The city, meanwhile, was spreading, both institutionally and in terms of settlement. The foundation of monasteries on the banks of the Seine, beyond the Île de la Cité, led to the development of suburbs near them – a process that was made considerably less risky by the cessation of Viking siege attempts after 885–6. However, it was only after the mid-tenth century that there was much expansion beyond the Île de la Cité on both sides of the Seine. Despite the usual problems of densely populated, insanitary cities – disease, and difficulties with food supplies – the economy continued to grow.

The continued importance of the French crown (as distinct from the more varied position of individual monarchs) ensured that the capital was significant, and under the Capetians, from 987, it definitely became Paris rather than any other city. Widespread population increase and economic expansion characterized the eleventh, twelfth and thirteenth centuries. Trade increased, as it remained a key location for commerce on and across the Seine. There were docks at the Rue des Ursins on the Île de la Cité and, from the twelfth century, near the modern Hôtel de Ville. In response to the substantial uptick in activity and profits, there were changes to the city's infrastructure. The centre of trade was on the north bank of the Seine, but thanks to royal support in the twelfth century, a commercial fair from outside Paris moved to a new site at the north-west edge of the city; it became the anchor for a new commercial centre between there and the bridge crossing to the governmental centre on the Île de la Cité. The Pont au Change or Money-Changers' Bridge, constructed in the ninth century by Charles the Bald, held a formal money exchange from 1141. This and other bridges typically supported numerous buildings (which possibly contributed to the collapse of the Pont Notre-Dame in 1499); streets developed as extensions of the bridges.

Paris controlled much of the Seine and other rivers in the sense of being exempt from tolls, but unlike many cities in Italy and Germany, it did not gain territorial control over lands. The role of the river was linked to the growing significance of its merchants for the governance of the city, although this remained very much under royal control. It was far easier and cheaper to transport goods by river than overland, especially for bulky materials like the large quantities of wood that were required for building, heating and industrial processes. The Seine had various important tributaries in and around Paris that have now, as with the Thames in London, been covered up. One of these is the Bièvre, which was used by boatmen and tanners before being covered in the eighteenth century – it leaves its mark in the Rue de Bièvre, near where it joins the Seine.

The kingdom of France grew more powerful under Philip Augustus (r. 1180–1223), who drove King John of England out of Anjou and Normandy. Philip's dynamism and success attracted more resources to the capital and he was generally keen on maintaining good relations with the towns so that they looked to the Crown rather than to the nobility, which served as a natural check on the power of the latter. He enhanced Paris by constructing a major wall from 1190 to 1215 and beginning work on the Louvre (as a fort); he also granted a charter to the university in 1200 and did much to develop Les Halles, a market established by Louis VI in 1135. Philip provided it with permanent buildings in 1183.

Paris in 1200 probably began to overtake London in population, but there are no precise figures. The wall constructed by Philip enclosed 273 hectares. Much of it was on the Right Bank, but on both it included land not hitherto developed and therefore provided a basis for further growth. Unlike in London, the palace was in the centre of the city. The expansion of the French state and the position of Paris at the focus of a river network served to ensure growth for the city at the expense of Rouen, which was lower down the Seine and better placed for maritime trade.

There was still a great deal of church-building, much of it linked to the division of the city into territorial parishes in the twelfth century. The Gothic style, which developed as a conscious rejection of the Romanesque, owed much to the Paris of Abbot Suger and particularly to the buildings of the 1130s. Paris would become a major centre of the Gothic: the dedication of the new choir of Saint-Denis in 1144 was a key inspiration, and Notre-Dame (begun in 1163 and completed in 1345, although it was largely finished by 1260, see plate III) was a masterpiece of architectural geometry. Its combination of the rib vault and the flying buttress provided a structural background for expansive window spaces displaying didactic stained glass. Many other historic Parisian church buildings date from this period; for example, Saint-Julien-le-Pauvre, which preserves its Gothic vaulting. Meanwhile, the schools of Paris were being united into a university (the model for English universities) with the encouragement of Philip Augustus and the support of the dynamic Pope Innocent III.

Paris was transforming into a leading intellectual centre not only of France, but of Western Europe. The development of a number of schools in the city was important, not least for the French church. In part this was driven by the general expansion of the city, which created a need for more housing and employment opportunities; but it also owed much to the support of individuals like William of Champeaux, who in 1108 founded the canonry and school of Saint-Victor, winning royal patronage. It served as a key educational site on the Left Bank; the Latin Quarter took its name from the use of the language in this neighbourhood, strong in both academic and religious activity.

Notre-Dame had a cathedral school that was particularly notable from the twelfth century, with a revival then in the study of Roman law and classical philosophy as well as the systematization of canon law and theology. The achievements of the twelfth-century Renaissance owed much to Paris. Essentially optimistic, this humanism assumed benign purpose, knowability and the possibility of aligning human life with both divine creation and the intention expressed in this creation. Ideas of knowability were linked to the development of scientific empiricism in works by William of Conches and Thierry of Chartres. Their arguments in favour of a method that combined induction with deductive thought were related to a new readiness to accept contingent and changing results rather than clear-cut certainty. Looking towards the arguments of Parisian thinkers during the Enlightenment of the eighteenth century, doubt – to be clarified by information deployed by a God-given human intellect – was crucial in the assertion of this new rationalism. However, in the thirteenth century the university became a focus for Scholasticism, a systematic rationalism that did not welcome doubt.

The study of mathematics and what would later be termed science led, in the fourteenth century, to the development by Jean Buridan of ideas relevant to what would eventually be called 'momentum' and 'inertia'. Also at the University of Paris around this time, Nicole Oresme was working on the mean speed theorem and plotting the speed of an object against time. The work of these remarkably original thinkers set the stage for the later theories and research of Copernicus and Galileo.

Under Louis IX (Saint Louis, r. 1226–70) there was much support for the church, including continued church-building – notably the building of the Sainte-Chapelle (see plate IV), which was designed to house the sacred relics he collected. Consecrated in 1248, the church has great windows of stained glass through which light would have shone on the reliquary shrine, positioned on a raised platform at the centre of the apse; it remained there until it was destroyed during the Revolution. Louis's sister, Saint Isabelle, founded Longchamp Abbey in a location near the present-day racecourse of the same name. As with many such sites, little remains bar, in this case, a tower.

As the capital, Paris was also the scene of various unpleasant incidents of religious intolerance. In 1240–2, at a 'trial' in Paris, rabbis were obliged to deny charges that the Talmud insulted Christianity; in 1242, large numbers of the books were burned in the city. Although each episode was unique to its particular circumstances, there are instructive parallels between episodes of antisemitism across the city's history.

Growth on both banks of the Seine has been consistent throughout the last millennium of Paris's history, as there is no fundamental barrier to expansion in any direction. In the medieval period this growth brought with it a measure of specialization, with educational and religious activity more prominent on the Left Bank (where the university was situated) and industrial and commercial activity on the right. The Rue des Lombards became a centre for banking, its name reflecting the role of Italians. There were improvements in infrastructure: streets were paved and wooden bridges upgraded to stone. Administration became more sophisticated with the establishment of the position of Provost in 1260 and the formalization of guild statutes – these innovations represented a form of municipal self-government in keeping with a broader

European pattern, although there was continued royal oversight. Paris was also established as the centre and setting of royal governance and politics. Thus, the *lit de justice* – a ceremonial visit by the king to the *parlement* of Paris – became more important from the 1320s onwards, symbolizing cooperation between the monarch and the *parlement*.

The burning end of the Templars

THE VIOLENT SUPPRESSION OF THE FABULOUSLY WEALTHY TEMPLAR Crusading Order in 1307–14 by Philip IV (known as *le roi de fer*, the Iron King) culminated in the burning at the stake of many Templars on trumped-up charges of idolatry, conveniently wiping out Philip's enormous debts to the Order. While being burned alive in 1314, Jacques de Molay, Grand Master of the Knights Templar, called out his defiance of the king and Pope Clement V: 'Soon a calamity will occur to those who have condemned us to death.'

Philip had ordered the arrest of the Knights in 1307, then set about extracting confessions under torture. From 1310 the executions began, and in 1312, under pressure from Philip, Clement abolished the Order (which was in theory answerable only to him, a fact Philip had always resented). The Catholic Church now admits that the persecution was unjust.

The burning took place on the Île aux Juifs, which was just to the west of the Île de la Cité and was later joined to it by the construction of the Pont Neuf. A number of Jews had been executed on the island. There is a marker at the site of de Molay's execution, beside the stairs from the Pont Neuf Bridge.

In 1300, Paris was the sixth most populous city in the world (and the sole European city in the top ten), surpassed only by four Chinese cities and Cairo. Byzantium, its most obvious rival, had been hit very hard by the Fourth Crusade in 1204. Paris, as a city, was the capital of a state that wielded more power than any other in Western Europe. It was also no longer in the shadow of Rome.

Chapter 3

Later Medieval Paris

The Hôtel de Sens, located on a quiet street in the 4th arron-dissement near where the Marais meets the Seine, is not one of Paris's better-known tourist sites, but it is an impressive building. One of the city's few surviving medieval private residences, it was built between 1475 and 1507 for the influential Archbishop of Sens. It displays a number of characteristically medieval Gothic features that, elsewhere in Paris, have largely been swept away by later rebuilding: turrets, a castellated tower, a spiral staircase. The better-known Musée de Cluny is based around a building of the same period – a time of relative stability in the wake of prolonged turbulence.

In the mid-fourteenth century, Paris had entered a period of crisis whose impact has only ever been matched by the sixteenth-century Wars of Religion and the German occupation of the Second World War. Even compared to those, the crisis that began in the 1340s was unmatched in its duration, lasting until the 1430s. It started with what is sometimes oversimplified as an epidemic of bubonic plague in 1348–50; in reality there was a more varied and more sustained series of epidemics, made all the more serious by the impact of global cooling on agricultural yields and on human and animal health. Following a number of earlier epidemics with various causes (in 1317, 1323, 1328, 1334 and 1340–41), that of 1348–50 was the deadliest of all, wiping out about a third of Paris's population. The terrible impact of disease on the labour force was compounded by war with Edward III of England: this was an early stage of the Hundred Years' War, which began in 1337 and turned disastrous for France following major defeats at Crécy (1346) and Poitiers (1356).

Rural uprisings had long affected the supply of food to Paris, particularly during the Great Famine of 1315–17. In 1356–8, there was disorder as Étienne Marcel, Provost of the Merchants of Paris, attempted to pursue reform and public control of the government and was met with opposition from the nobility. In an atmosphere of increasing violence, he was assassinated in 1358; he is commemorated by a nineteenth-century statue by Antonin Idrac in the Hôtel de Ville.

There followed a breathing space as peace with Edward was negotiated in 1360, and during the late fourteenth century there was an understandable emphasis on improving the city's defences against both external and internal threats. Charles V (r. 1364–80) drove forward the construction of a ring of impressive walls, which would be supplemented in the late sixteenth century by earthen bastions. The Bastille was built, partly by forced labour, in 1370–82; Charles also expanded the Louvre, turning Philip Augustus's fortress into a royal palace. He built another palace at the Hôtel Saint-Pol, which was protected by the Bastille and thought to be relatively safe from the diseases of the crowded city. This is one of many palaces that are now no more: abandoned after 1418, it was demolished in the 1520s.

A golden sceptre made for Charles V is held in the Louvre. He also began building a palace at Vincennes, east of Paris, in an

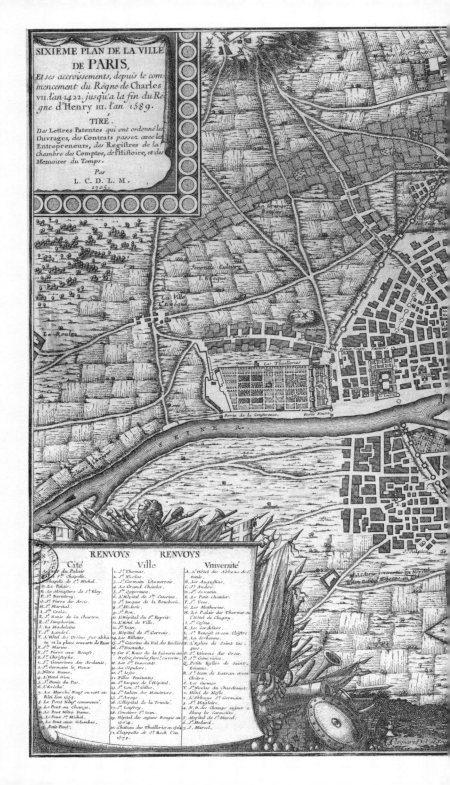

SIXIEME PLAN DE LA VILLE
DE PARIS,
Et ses accroissements, depuis le com-
mencement du Règne de Charles
VII. l'an 1422. jusqu'a la fin du Rè-
gne d'Henry III. l'an 1589.
TIRÉ.
Des Lettres Patentes qui ont ordonné les
Ouvrages, des Contrats passez avec les
Entrepreneurs, des Registres de la
Chambre des Comptes, de l'Histoire, et des
Memoires du Temps.
Par
L. C. D. L. M.
1705.

La Grange Bateliere

Seconde Culture l'Eveque

La Ville l'Eveque

Le Roule

Les Thuilleries

Porte de la Conference. Porte Neuve.

SEINE R.

RENVOYS — RENVOYS

Cité

A. La Cour du Palais
B. La S.te Chapelle.
C. Chapelle de S.t Michel.
D. Le Palais.
E. Le Monastere de S.t Eloy.
F. S.t Barthelemy.
G. S.t Pierre des Arcis.
H. S.t Martial.
I. S.te Croix.
K. S.t Denis de la Chartre.
R. S.t Simphorien.
I. La Madeleine.
T. S.t Landri.
L. L'Hôtel de Ville fut abba-
tu et la place couverte de Ruës
F. S.t Marine.
Y. S.t Pierre aux Boeufs.
S. S.t Christophe.
4. S.te Genevieve des Ardents.
2. S.t Germain le Vieux.
3. Nôtre Dame.
4. L'Hôtel Dieu.
5. S.t Denis du Pas.
6. L'Eveché.
7. Le Marché Neuf ouvert et
bâti l'an 1555.
8. Le Pont Neuf commencé.
9. Le Pont au Change.
10. Le Pont Nôtre Dame.
11. Le Pont S.t Michel.
12. Le Pont aux Colombes.
13. Petit Pont.

Ville

1. S.t Thomas.
2. S.t Nicolas.
3. S.t Germain l'Auxerrois.
4. Le Grand Chastelet.
5. S.t Opportune.
6. L'Hôpital de S.te Caterine.
7. S.t Jacque de la Boucherie.
8. S.t Merderie.
9. S.t Ron.
10. L'Hôpital du S.t Esprit.
11. L'Hôtel de Ville.
12. S.t Jean.
13. S.t Gervais.
14. Les Billettes.
15. S.te Caterine de Val des Ecoliers
16. S.t Eustache.
17. Les 6.e Ruës de la Juiverie ou
triesse fermées furent ouvertes.
18. Les S.ts Innocents.
19. Le Sepulere.
20. S.t Lazare.
21. Filles Penitentes.
22. S.t Jacques de l'Hôpital.
23. S.t Leu S.t Gilles.
24. S.t Julien des Ménetriers.
25. S.t Avoye.
26. L'Hôpital de la Trinité.
27. S.t Laffroy.
28. Cimetiere S.t Jean.
29. Hôpital des enfans Rouge en
1536.
30. Chateau des Thuilleries en 1564.
31. Chappelle de S.t Roch l'an
1578.

Vniversité

A. L'Hôtel des Abbez de S.t
Denis.
B. Les Augustins.
C. S.t André.
D. S.t Severin.
E. Le Petit Chastelet.
F. S.t Yves.
G. Les Mathurins.
H. Le Palais des Thermes ou
l'Hôtel de Clugny.
I. Cisne.
K. Les Cordeliers.
L. S.t Benoist et son Cloître.
M. La Sorbonne.
N. L'Eglise de Saint Jac-
ques.
O. S.t Etienne des Grecs.
P. S.te Genevieve.
Q. Petite Eglise de Saint
Etienne.
R. S.t Jean de Latran avec son
Clôitre.
S. Les Carmes.
T. S.t Nicolas du Chardonnet.
1. Hôtel de Nesle.
2. L'Abbaye S.t Germain.
3. S.t Magloire.
4. N.D. des Champs séjour ou
Abaye des Carmelites.
5. Hôpital de S.t Marcel.
6. S.t Medard.
7. S.t Marcel.

S.t Sulpice

Maladrerie convertie en Hôpital
S.t Jean Baptiste Malcou

Cognard f.

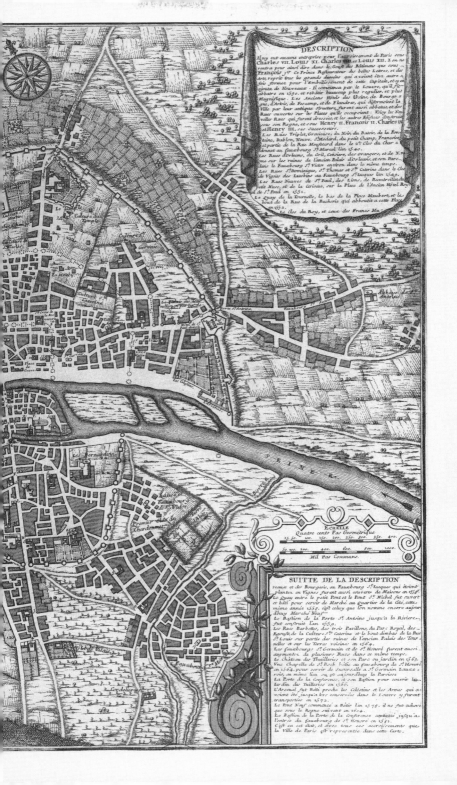

area with good hunting. It included a chapel inspired by Sainte-Chapelle in the city and intended, similarly, to hold a collection of relics; Henry V of England would die there in 1422. The chapel remained unfinished until the mid-sixteenth century, only being dedicated in 1552, and its window spaces provided an opportunity for the impressive use of stained glass.

Charles VI (r. 1380–1422) was a less successful ruler than his predecessor, particularly when it came to confronting disorder in Paris. In 1382, opposition to increased taxation in the wake of war and plague led to the Maillotin uprising (as it had in England to the Peasants' Revolt the previous year). In Paris, the fighting began in Les Halles: tax collectors were killed and there was widespread looting, as well as violence directed towards Jewish residents. With the royal forces unable to restore order, government collapsed – but the royal army then blocked traffic on the Seine, stopping food supplies from getting through. In order to get on top of the situation, repeal and amnesty were agreed, but once royal forces gained entry to the city the rebel leaders were seized and executed.

Further lasting division was caused by the inability of Charles, who was mentally ill from about 1393, to control his quarrelsome aristocratic family members, the Dukes of Orléans and Burgundy. In a French counterpart to England's Wars of the Roses, the ascendant Orléans party, later known as the Armagnacs, were challenged in 1405 by a display of power at Paris by John the Fearless, Duke of Burgundy. Louis I, the king's brother and Duke of Orléans, was murdered in 1407 on Rue Vieille-du-Temple, having been tricked into believing that the king wanted to see him. Backed by much of the city's population, Burgundy then seized power. He also added in 1409–11 a fortified tower, the Tour Jean-sans-Peur, to his Parisian town palace; it served as his headquarters and is still visible today on the Rue Étienne-Marcel.

Both sides raised armies, and there was fighting in the Paris suburbs in 1410–11. In 1413 the situation blew up into the Cabochien revolt, in which tradesmen led by butchers attacked Armagnac nobles, executed the provost, and brought about a bloody period of anarchy – only for the Cabochiens to be overthrown in an Armagnac-backed popular reaction later that year. In 1418, Paris was taken over by the Burgundians in their turn and the Armagnac leaders were killed.

This ongoing rumble of civil warfare took place against a back-drop of international crisis caused by Henry V of England's invasion in 1415 and his dramatic victory over the French at Agincourt. The murder of Duke John in 1419 by the Royalists at what was supposed to be a negotiation led the Burgundians to turn to Henry, whose forces entered the city in 1420. That year, having married Charles's daughter, Henry was recognized as his heir and as regent during his life. When Henry died of dysentery in 1422 he was succeeded by his baby son, Henry VI, who was crowned king of France in 1430 in Paris – from which Charles VII, the rival claimant and son of Charles VI, had been kept the previous year, when an unsuc-cessful attempt to storm the Porte Saint-Honoré led to Joan of Arc (see plate II) being wounded in the leg by a crossbow bolt. The Parisians under Simon Mohier, the provost, and Jean de Villiers, the governor, were responsible for the defence and fought bravely, repelling attacks by larger forces.

Today there are four statues of Joan in Paris – in the Place des Pyramides, where she was wounded, the Rue de la Chapelle, the Place Saint-Augustin and the Boulevard Saint-Marcel – but at the time, this defeat served to discredit her with the royal court. Her questioning of Charles VII's command of the siege was unwelcome;

her desire to fight clashed with his politics of seeking reconciliation with Burgundy; and her failure at Paris led to the claim that her inspiration was not divine. After being captured by the Burgundians she was transferred to the English, convicted of heresy and burnt at the stake in Rouen. Most of the clerics who participated in her trial were linked to the University of Paris, which approved the charges of heresy.

Control over Paris continued to be hotly contested. A plot on behalf of Charles VII, discovered in 1430, led to the hanging of six Parisians, while attempts by his forces to gain access in 1432 and 1434 were thwarted. However, the situation altered when Philip the Good, Duke of Burgundy, switched sides in 1435 with the Treaty of Arras. This led to a sea change in Paris, with Jean de Villiers also turning to Charles VII, which weakened the English position in the city.

Once regained from the English in 1436, Paris again served as capital for the Valois kings – although they spent scant time there, in part because the city did not seem safe. Charles VII (r. 1422–61) established his capital at Bourges for part of his reign and although he entered Paris in triumph in 1437, he still spent his subsequent reign outside it, dying at Mehun-sur-Yèvre in central France. This absence of a court and all its attendant wealth, which continued until 1528, was bad for the city's economy. Louis XI (r. 1461–83), born in Bourges in 1423, preferred not Paris but nearby Vincennes, where, again, he was more secure.

As France drove out the English and absorbed new territory, including Burgundy in the late 1470s, so Paris gained in significance both governmentally and economically; among other things, the city now had more than a hundred guilds covering a broad range of craft skills. And with the passing of the lengthy crisis came other developments in culture: the dialect of the Paris region, *francien*, dominated in northern France, and three printing presses imported from Mainz in 1469 were installed at the Sorbonne as the basis of the nation's first printing operation. The city, like the country, was changing.

Chapter 4

The Sixteenth Century

Paris has seen countless rapid changes of fortune in the course of its long history; indeed, this is one of the characteristics that sets it apart from London or New York. The 1560s certainly brought major changes. Many decades had passed since the city had last been a royal residence of note, but now, during the Wars of Religion, its position altered radically and it acquired a new importance for the Crown. Prior to this, from as early as the 1520s, there had already been action there against Protestants.

Religious dissent from the Catholic Church had developed in Paris during the 1510s, 1520s and 1530s, and firm disciplinary action had been taken. Jacques Lefèvre, a humanist-inclined priest educated at the University of Paris, was based in the abbey of Saint-Germain-des-Prés from 1507 to 1520, but his approach to the study of the Bible was controversial. His translation of the New Testament into French in 1523 was banned, although Francis I (r. 1515–47) protected him when the *parlement* of Paris acted against him in 1525. Theologian John Calvin, who was also educated for a while in Paris, fled in 1533 when his friend Nicolas Cop, the university rector, was accused of heresy after pressing for clerical reform. The 'Affair of the Placards' in 1534, when posters appeared in Paris and other cities attacking Catholic concepts of the Eucharist, prompted a determined response: religious processions took place all across Paris, and Protestants were arrested and burnt at the stake. This practice had previously been employed in 1523 to kill Jean Vallière, a monk accused of supporting the teachings of Martin Luther, who had been condemned by the Sorbonne in 1521.

Francis I became hostile to Protestants after the Affair of the Placards, ensuring that the Paris *parlement* and the theologians of the Sorbonne were given their head. In 1546, an early Unitarian called Étienne Dolet was convicted of heresy and killed in the Place Maubert, close to the Sorbonne. His books were also burned there. A bronze statue of him was erected in 1889 during the Third Republic, only to be removed by the Germans and melted down in 1942. Tensions over Protestantism in Paris became even more marked under Henry II (r. 1547–59), particularly from 1557, when he issued the harsh Edict of Compiègne and a mob attacked a Calvinist meeting in Paris.

In 1562, during the First War of Religion, Francis, Duke of Guise, the most prominent Catholic aristocrat, intimidated Charles IX (r. 1560–74) into returning to Paris from Fontainebleau. The later advance of the Huguenots (French Protestants) under the Prince of Condé was thwarted when Guise reinforced the city and was victorious at Dreux. In 1567, during the Second War, the Huguenots blockaded Paris.

In 1572 Paris became a crucible of tension during a brief period of peace. Concern about the intentions of Admiral Coligny, Condé's replacement, combined with popular anti-Protestantism in a city that was preponderantly Catholic, resulted in a volatile atmosphere. An attempt on Coligny's life at the behest of the Guises in late August led to fears of further religious warfare. To preempt this, Charles IX and his council apparently decided to assassinate the Huguenot leaders.

1, The Pilier des Nautes was discovered in 1711 in the foundations of Notre-Dame Cathedral. The column is Gallo-Roman and was erected in honour of Jupiter by Gallic sailors of the Parisii tribe during the first century CE.

11, Depictions of Joan of Arc can be found across Paris, including four statues and various artistic interpretations, here Joan is depicted as part of a historical initial in a fifteenth century illuminated manuscript.

III, TOP Built during the late twelfth century, Notre-Dame de Paris, meaning 'Our Lady of Paris', is one of the most visited monuments in the world and was designated a UNESCO World Heritage Site in 1991.

IV, ABOVE Sainte-Chapelle was commissioned by Louis IX and completed in 1248. It was designed to house the relics he collected and originally contained twenty-two artefacts; only three remain, now housed in Notre-Dame Cathedral.

v, *Le massacre de la Saint-Barthélemy* (The Saint Bartholomew's Day Massacre)
by François Dubois, 1572–84, depicts the Catholic mob violence against the Protestant
Huguenots that erupted in Paris during the Wars of Religion in 1572.

VI, OPPOSITE ABOVE Portrait of Louis XIV in his military regalia by Claude Lefèbvre, c. 1670.

VII, OPPOSITE BELOW The Hall of Mirrors at the palace of Versailles was designed by the architect Jules Hardouin-Mansart and completed in 1684; it measures 73 metres (240 feet) long, contains 357 mirrors and took 6 years to build.

VIII, ABOVE Louis XV in sacred costume by Louis-Michel van Loo, c. 1763. Louis was a major patron of architecture and the arts. Many believe that his reign was the period when Paris reached its artistic and cultural zenith.

IX, *Marie Antoinette en gaulle* after Élisabeth Vigée Le Brun, 1783. The original portrait was first displayed at a Salon exhibition, causing a scandal, with many shocked that the queen had been depicted in such informal attire. The painting was removed and Le Brun provided an alternative portrait.

A city for satire

CONDEMNED IN 1533 BY THE SORBONNE AS OBSCENE, *THE TERRIBLE Deeds and Acts of Prowess of Pantagruel, King of the Dipsodes* (1532) by François Rabelais, a priest, includes a fantastical attack on the scholars of the University of Paris as well as an account of lecherous Parisian roguery in the person of Panurge, a pickpocket:

> ...he had a great many little horns full of fleas and lice, which he borrowed from the beggars of St. Innocent, and cast them with small canes or quills to write with into the necks of the daintiest gentlewomen that he could find....he used to have a good store of hooks and buckles, wherewith he would couple men and women together that sat in company close to one another, but especially those that wore gowns of crimson taffeties, that, when they were about to go away, they might rend all their gowns.—Trans. Thomas Urquhart and Peter Antony Motteux

The killing of some leading Protestants on St Bartholomew's Eve (the night of 23–24 August) was followed by a widespread massacre of Paris's Huguenot population by Catholics (see plate v). The slaughter, in which more than 2,000 people were murdered, represented a total breakdown in civic relations, with neighbours killing neighbours at close quarters; it triggered the outbreak of the Fourth War of Religion. It has been depicted many times over by writers and artists, as such extreme events often are – from Christopher Marlowe's play *The Massacre at Paris* (1593) to Giacomo Meyerbeer's opera *Les Huguenots* (1836), a smash hit of its time and

ORIENS

DEVERS IS

Icy est le vray pourtraict naturel de la ville, cité, vniuersité
& Fauxbourgs de Paris, ou sont fidelement figurées toutes les Rues & Ruelles, corespondans les
vne à l'autre, ainsi qu'elles sont de present situées, qui sont en nõbre deux cens quatre vingts &
sept. Pareillement sont figurées toutes les Eglises, & Monastères, qui sont en nombre cent
quatre. Aussi sont figurées tous les Collèges, qui sont en nõbre quarante neuf. Et pour con-
gnoistre iceulx Rues, Ruelles, Eglises, Monastères & Collèges, vous trouuerez leurs noms
au reng à chascun selon son propre endroict. Cõme plus amplement vous pouez voir cy dessus.

A Paris, par Oliuier Truchet, & Germain Hoyau, demourans en
la Rue de Montorgueil, au Chef sainct Denys.

the first opera to receive more than 1,000 performances at the Paris Opéra. Voltaire, who was appalled by the type of prejudice that led to the massacre, claimed to be ill on its anniversary each year.

The Massacre at Paris

CHRISTOPHER MARLOWE'S PLAY *THE MASSACRE AT PARIS* BROUGHT the events of St Bartholomew's Day 1572 vividly to life on stage, with the villain, Henry I, the Duke of Guise, made a hysterical murderer:

> They that shall be actors in this massacre
> Shall wear white crosses on their burgonets,
> And tie white linen scarfs about their arms;
> He that wants these, and is suspected of heresy,
> Shall die, be he king or emperor.
> Then I'll have a peal of ordnance shot from the tower,
> At which they all shall issue out, and set the streets,
> And then, the watchword being given, a bell shall ring,
> Which when they hear, they shall begin to kill,
> And never cease until that bell shall cease;
> Then breathe a while.
> ...Let none escape! Murder the Huguenots!
> ...Stab him, I say, and send him to his friends in hell.
> ...Murder the Huguenots!

In 1589, Charles IX's brother and successor, Henry III (r. 1574–89) – who, somewhat ironically, had previously been more keen than earlier monarchs to keep the royal court in Paris – was assassinated by a Dominican friar at Saint-Cloud while besieging the city. The previous year, Henry's impressive Swiss Guards had been driven out by the Catholic League and the city militia on the so-called Day of the Barricades, when barrels (*barriques*) had been filled with earth and stones; Henry had fled to Chartres. Early in 1589, at the Louvre, his furniture and collections had been destroyed and his great seal symbolically broken.

In 1590, his Protestant successor Henry IV (the first king of the Bourbon dynasty; *r.* 1589–1610), who had narrowly escaped death in the massacre of St Bartholomew's Eve, besieged Paris. The privations of the siege were harsh, with many dying of starvation, but the city was eventually relieved by a Spanish army that had advanced from the Netherlands.

In November 1591 Catholic radicals seized power and executed a leading moderate, the president of the *parlement* of Paris, provoking a show of force by Charles, Duke of Mayenne, a Guise who was the leader of the Catholic League. His response included the execution of four of the radicals as well as the takeover of the bourgeois militia, the largest military body in Paris not under royal or aristocratic control. Officers loyal to Mayenne were appointed while soldiers of humble status, and therefore not entitled to belong to the militia, were disarmed.

In order to gain Paris, Henry IV was famously obliged to renounce his faith and embrace Catholicism in 1593; he is said to have remarked, 'Paris is well worth a mass.' He was crowned the following February, and he and Mayenne made their peace in 1595.

Meanwhile, over the course of the sixteenth century, the city's population had continued to grow: it reached about 250,000 by 1564, and would soar to 500,000 by 1640. Despite decades of warfare during which the French kings, notably Francis I, spent much time at their palaces in the Loire Valley – where the hunting was better, they felt safer and were closer to the Italian battlefields – the capital did see some development, especially after Francis began to spend more time there from 1528. He made major changes to the Louvre, where he lived, and built a hunting lodge in the Bois de Boulogne as well as commissioning a new city hall, the Hôtel de Ville. The Collège Royal was founded around this period too, and a royal arsenal was constructed south of the Bastille to produce munitions – this was blown up in 1563, but later rebuilt. Francis's son, Henry II, spent more time in the capital than his father and also built in the Louvre; the *Salle des Cariatides*, with its four large statues supporting an upper gallery, was completed during his reign.

Chapter 5

The Seventeenth Century

The Merian map of Paris, produced in 1615 and shown in this chapter, enables us to see both the city of the early seventeenth century and its medieval legacy. Swiss-born Matthäus Merian (1593–1650) was a noted mapmaker who produced engravings offering panoramic views of cities. In the cartouche at the bottom left of the map, he offers a verse to the reader:

> *This city is another world*
> *Therein a flowerful world,*
> *Of people very powerful*
> *to whom all things abound.*

Merian's map captures the stabilization of Paris and indeed France under Henry IV (r. 1589–1610), who had secured in 1598 both the end of the Wars of Religion and peace with Spain. Oriented to the east, the panoramic view suggests the proximity of the countryside, although Paris itself, as the largest city in Europe, seemed an urban phenomenon to contemporaries both French and foreign. The map also shows the river busy with ships, as it certainly was.

Some of the structures that were built around this time and included on the map remain key to the appearance of Paris as we see it today. The Pont Neuf, begun in 1578 but only completed in 1606, was the city's first stone bridge as well as the first not to be topped with buildings. With nothing to block the view, this style of bridge was able to offer a grand prospect. Where the bridge crossed the Île de la Cité, a bronze equestrian statue of Henry was erected in 1618 opposite the grand Place Dauphine.

Henry also linked the Tuileries Palace (built in the previous century) to the Louvre by means of a long Grande Galerie, parallel to the Seine. Among other functions it served as a space for the royal princes to take indoor exercise, and as an escape route from the city. Further east, he supported the construction of the Place Royale, a symmetrical square made distinctive by the identical façades lining each of its four sides (since 1800, it has been known as the Place des Vosges). In the 1610s the ditch between the rural islands east of the Île de la Cité, previously used for grazing and for sourcing wood, was filled in and the land built over, becoming the Île Saint-Louis. With a similar process taking place to the west, the city was ceasing to be a watery realm with small islands in its centre – it was being stabilized.

On his way to campaign against Spanish forces in the Lower Rhineland Henry was assassinated by François Ravaillac, a Catholic zealot, in his carriage on Rue de la Ferronnerie in 1610 (an occasion marked there by a commemorative slab). His widow, Marie de Medici, became a major figure in the reign of their son Louis XIII (r. 1610–43). As she disliked the Louvre she built the Luxembourg Palace on the other bank, modelling it on the Palazzo Pitti in her native Florence. Its gardens – which also showed Tuscan influence, notably in the Medici Fountain (1624) – remain one of the city's most pleasant places.

Le Plan de la Ville Cité Vn

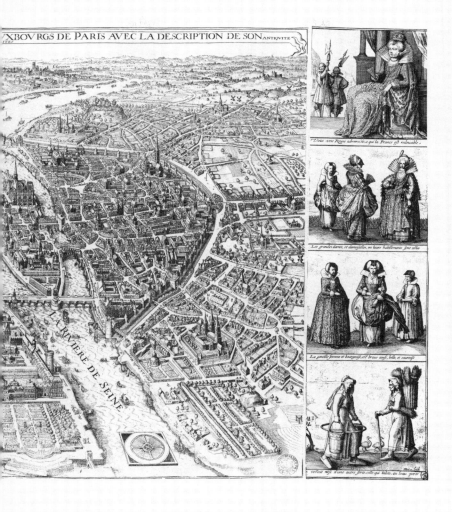

Under Louis XIII there was an expansion of housing in the Faubourg Saint-Germain, the Île Saint-Louis and the Marais, as well as work on a new city wall. From 1616–21 the church of Saint-Gervais-Saint-Protais was rebuilt, acquiring the first French example of the superimposition of the three classical orders: Doric, Ionic and Corinthian. New institutions included the Académie Française and the Imprimerie Royale. Cardinal Richelieu, Louis's leading minister, displayed his commitment to the city by building the Palais-Cardinal (from 1643 the Palais-Royal). The king was celebrated in a statue erected there in 1639.

Parisian construction techniques, however, did not impress all visitors. One British traveller recalled that, 'using no putty, they fit their panes with paper and paste, which, with the soil of flies and dust of the streets, takes off the beauty…and has indeed a beggarly look'. There was a considerable degree of truth to this observation.

Protestantism in Paris had been crushed by the massacre in 1572 and the chaos of the Wars of Religion had largely been left behind. Although there was still religious conflict in France during the 1620s, it was focused on the southern and western regions, with a notable and eventually successful siege of the Huguenot stronghold of La Rochelle. In Paris, rather than incessant religious violence, there was now church-building and Catholic activism associated with the Catholic or Counter-Reformation, which had begun the previous century.

This activism is usually discussed in terms of the Church, and more particularly the Jesuits. There was certainly an active sharpening of clerical behaviour as reforms were introduced and implemented. At the same time the Catholic Reformation in Paris, as elsewhere, entailed much lay activity, with fraternities engaged in devotion and charitable work such as the provision of poor relief and education, or women's activism. This was in many respects the continuation of a pattern that had been established during the Middle Ages and disrupted by the Wars of Religion. It was to continue as an important element of Parisian life, despite the further disruption of the Revolution.

This aspect of Parisian history is sometimes overlooked owing to an understandable popular interest in the new and in radical tendencies – Enlightenment intellectuals in the eighteenth century, republicans and socialists in the nineteenth, or a secular narrative for the twentieth. However, it is important to remember that, while significant, those are merely a part of the whole picture. Furthermore, the Church–society nexus was not simply a reactionary monolith gradually eroded by the flow of change but, instead, a force of dynamism, capable itself of development as well as continuity, and grounded in the localities of Paris, its parishes and its churches. This nexus continued to play a political role in the twentieth century, lending resilience to conservatism in a number of forms, including Gaullism and support for church schools.

But religion played no significant part in the rebellion that broke out in Paris in 1648. It was one of several mid-century rebellions across Europe in response to the individual circumstances of different states, as well as to international events. The impact of a series of wars on public finances, taxation and politics was very serious. So also were the consequences of the crisis in living standards related to the 'Little Ice Age', a prolonged period of global cooling that was affecting agricultural productivity.

The conflict known as the *Fronde parlementaire*, focusing on Paris and opposition to the royal government by the *parlement* of Paris, took its name from the French for 'sling'; slings were used by the rioters who took control of the city, which was bisected by barricades in response to proposals for new taxation. The government gave way but the end of the Thirty Years' War in Germany, which meant that France was no longer at war with the Austrian Habsburgs, helped the Crown regain the initiative – a process encouraged by division between Parisian and aristocratic opposition. A peace in 1649 was followed by fresh rebellion in 1650 as a consequence of the breakdown in relations between the government and aristocrats who turned for help to Spain. Disorder continued until 1652, when, after fresh differences between the Parisians and the aristocrats, Louis XIV (*r.* 1642–1715) made a ceremonial re-entry to the city at the head of his guards (see plate VI).

Thereafter, although Paris had defied and expelled royal forces in 1588 and 1648, it did not do so again until 1789. In part, this relative stability reflected a rebuilding of the social and political connections between crown and nobility that had been driven to failure, sparking rebellion, during the Wars of Religion and then by the unpopular governance from 1624 to 1661 of the Cardinal Ministers, Richelieu and Mazarin. Royal patronage had come to be monopolized by a particular faction, leading to opposition and resistance by those who felt excluded.

Louis XIV sought to end all of this by dispensing with the idea of a powerful first minister. Indeed, in 1661 he imprisoned Nicolas Fouquet, the Parisian-born Superintendent of Finance and the prime contender for such a post. Fouquet's wealth can be readily seen today at Vaux-le-Vicomte, a palace that makes for a pleasant day trip from Paris without the crowds of Versailles.

Louis's extension of royal patronage was facilitated by a major expansion of the army, both peacetime and wartime, which provided many suitably high-status opportunities for the nobility. So too with the governance of the localities; Versailles in part reflected this reknitting of relations as aristocrats spent time there, making it an appropriate setting for the Crown and company for the king.

Any discussion of Versailles raises the question of how best to define both Paris and the changes in its position over time. The palace was not in the capital, but very much outside. In part this reflected the concerns about urban disorder, rebellion and disease that had affected earlier choices of residence, such as the Hôtel Saint-Pol and the château at Vincennes. Indeed, as a fortified position in the city's defences, the Louvre could originally have been seen in the same light; its transformation, culminating under Henry II, into a palace had led to the vulnerability seen with Henry III's expulsion from Paris, as well as the difficulties facing the young Louis XIV during the *Fronde*.

There was more at stake with Versailles, however, than the security provided by distance from the city or the troops that might be deployed in protection. The site offered the possibility of construction on a grand scale, including, crucially, gardens and grounds that would not have been feasible in the capital. As a consequence, Versailles was *of* Paris but not *in* it. It was part of the infrastructure of the capital – as, very differently, Charles de Gaulle Airport now is.

The location of the prime palace so close to the capital, incorporated into its political, governmental and social functions, influenced the movements of monarchs – or rather, their lack of movement. Of the three kings who ruled from 1643 to 1792, only Louis XIV spent much time outside Paris, and that was essentially on campaign in the Spanish Netherlands (now Belgium). His great-grandson, Louis XV, also went on campaign, but as neither man spent significant amounts of time elsewhere in France, the palaces of the Loire Valley slowly atrophied. Versailles was very much the dominant residence, although Louis XV also hunted at Compiègne.

Louis XVI did not go on campaign, and as king he only travelled outside the Paris area thrice: to Reims for his coronation, to
Cherbourg to view the harbour works, and to Varennes in 1791
on his unsuccessful attempt to flee the country.

This concentration of activity on Versailles forged an unprec-
edented link between ruler and Parisian location and led to a
fashion among the aristocracy for building residences in western
Paris, especially the south-west. There they could take advantage
of the expansion of the city as new residential areas were laid out,
but also of the proximity to Versailles. This was a change from
the earlier focus of the elite on the Marais, which had provided
residences into the mid-seventeenth century and offered access
to the palaces at the Hôtel Saint-Pol and Vincennes. Indeed, the
Marais now began a decline into a somewhat discarded part of
the city, although the fine houses and churches of the seventeenth
century continued to have a role into the eighteenth.

The palace provided endless opportunities for the display of
royal glory. The *Galerie des Glaces*, the largest long gallery yet built,
had ceiling paintings commemorating Louis's triumphs, notably in
the Dutch War of 1672–8. In the *Salon de la Guerre*, finished and
opened to the public in 1686, Antoine Coysevox presented Louis
as a stuccoed Mars, god of war. Engravings, medals and tapestries
spread images of glory and brought work and profit to the luxury
trades of Paris. Louis commissioned Gobelins tapestries to record
the public apologies made by Spain (1662) and the papacy (1664)
after clashes over precedence and recognition. Masques, plays and
operas focused on victories, with Philippe Quinault's libretto for
Lully's 1677 opera *Isis* presenting Louis as Neptune and referring
to recent Mediterranean successes. It was considered important
that the court opera at Versailles was more magnificent than the
Habsburg one at Vienna.

Although gatherings and etiquette were socially segregated, there were some social overlaps. These included residential proximity, with the humble living in the interstices of the great, as well as shared popular interests, such as watching public executions. The common amusements of the 'best people' and the rest were enjoyed in such places as the theatres at the numerous fairs held in Paris, which were frequented by the nobility as well as the lower orders.

The control of crime and disorder was key to the city's governance. When the *lieutenance de police*, founded in 1667, was reorganized in 1701 Paris acquired a strong permanent force of municipal police, including a detective section to gather intelligence and investigate crime. Compared to many cities it was well policed, with local criminals generally not having the resources to push back effectively against the work of the force. Indeed, on learning of the serious breakdown in public order in London during the Gordon Riots of 1780, the Paris-born writer Louis-Sébastien Mercier suggested that similar unrest was impossible in Paris – although he would, of course, be proved all too wrong when the Revolution began nine years later. A member of the National Convention, Mercier voted against the death penalty for Louis XVI and was imprisoned during the Reign of Terror, but survived to die in Paris in 1814.

In the meantime, despite the city being essentially well controlled, crime was still a problem. Violence and brutality were often to the fore – as George Carpenter wrote in 1717:

> …it is not safe to walk the streets after it is dark: there is seldom a night passes but somebody is found murdered. I was once persuaded by some company to go to see a criminal broke upon the wheel in this place, but had not resolution enough to stay it out.

Joseph Shaw, who witnessed a violent robbery from his window, wrote of 'nightly robberies and often murders committed'. In response, breaking the perpetrator alive on the wheel was one possible punishment for murder. A variety of capital punishments were carried out in the Place de Grève, known from 1830 as the Place de l'Hôtel de Ville.

Building in Paris during the reign of Louis XIV, with its repertoire of royal column, triumphal arch and monumental avenue, was designed to enhance the splendour of the monarchy as well as the capital. In royal iconography the monarchy symbolized France – a symbolism and ideological centrality that was pushed hard during this reign, but became less credible thereafter. Louis was at the centre of a cult of ornamental heroism, as reflected in the iconography and decoration of Versailles and also the Place Vendôme, a grand square laid out in 1702 incorporating a major equestrian statue of the king. The new Place des Victoires was also a display of Louis's triumph, with a statue of him crowned by Victory and trampling Cerberus, an image of discord, underfoot. This did not always go down well with outsiders. The Austrian envoy complained in 1686 to the French foreign minister that the Emperor (Leopold I):

> was not in the condition of a slave with his hands tied in chains…. This he thought fit to take notice of, upon occasion of one of the figures under the new statue, representing a slave in chains, with the arms of the Empire, the spread-eagle by him.

Louis was not an enthusiast for the *parlement* of Paris, the most important in France in terms of political and legal importance and area of jurisdiction. *Parlements* were final courts of appeal that had to register laws before they could take effect, and they had a right to criticize these laws through remonstrances. Between 1673 and 1713 Louis did not visit the *parlement*, and his solemn receptions for its delegates came to be defined as acts of extreme generosity on his part.

In 1670 – in an act that was bound to weaken Paris if it ever again became the centre of rebellion, as it had been in 1588 and 1648 – Louis demolished the fortified city walls, replacing them with *grands boulevards*. On the site of some of the former medieval gates he erected monuments including triumphal arches, the Portes Saint-Martin and Saint-Denis, celebrating his victories. William Mildmay, a British visitor, was to observe that 'all the gates of the city are only so many triumphal arches erected to his honour, on each of which the chiefest heroical acts of his reign are represented in fine basso relievo'.

God's triumph was also a theme, celebrated in the new convent and church of Val-de-Grâce, founded by Louis's mother in 1643, as well as the large Church of Saint-Roch, the foundation stone of which Louis laid in 1653, and the Église du Dôme, completed in 1708, its high gilded dome presiding over the Hôtel des Invalides that Louis ordered built in 1670 for wounded veterans. The defeat of the Huguenots was being followed by the reaffirmation of a Catholic cityscape and the strengthening of Catholic culture. Religious buildings dominated much of Paris, both visually and in terms of the space occupied; religious symbols such as crucifixes and shrines were frequent. There were many religious processions in the streets as well as large numbers of both religious and secular clergy (monks, nuns, and parish clergy).

There were also, of course, many religious paintings in the city, not only in churches but also in private collections. Charles Le Brun (1619–1690), who became Court Painter to Louis XIV in 1662 and played an important role in the founding of the Royal

Academy of Painting and Sculpture as well as the Gobelins tapestry works, produced not only paintings eulogizing the king but also works such as *The Sleep of Jesus* and *The Descent from the Cross*. John, Lord Perceval, a British visitor, was deeply affected by his *The Repentant Magdalen* (1655), now in the Louvre, but then in the Carmelite Church:

> ...inimitable for expression...fancy all the art of painting can do to express the most beautiful woman in tears and I need not spend time in commending the character, expression, colouring, drawing or the other parts which artists consider separately when they decide on pictures.

The flourishing of religious painting continued during the eighteenth century, although it is sometimes underappreciated due to the secular focus of much art commentary. Charles-André van Loo (1705–1765), who settled in Paris in 1734 and became First Painter to Louis XV in 1762, produced works including *Marriage of the Virgin* and *The Adoration of the Magi* as well as *St Charles Borromeo taking the Sacrament to the Plague Sufferers*, which William Drake saw at Notre-Dame:

> the zeal and sympathy of the good man, the extreme sickliness of the patient, who is brought out in her bed to receive the sacrament, the languishing of several other persons visited by this terrible calamity, are most naturally and inimitably expressed.

New building projects financed by Louis XIV included the Pont Royal across the Seine, built of stone in 1685–9 to replace a wooden bridge that had itself replaced a ferry. Building was also

Food for tourists

THE RANGE OF FOOD AVAILABLE IN PARIS WAS DESCRIBED BY THREE
English tourists who spent the summer of 1699 in the city:

> Paris and the other cities we saw are more populous than
> ours, their wine and bread finer than ours, they eat oftner
> than we do, and are more given to diversions and merriment
> than the English. Their butter, beer and cheese are not near
> so good as ours in England, and very little of them appears
> in their eating, as for their beef and veal, I think them not
> quite so good as the English, their veal especially is very
> bad, their rabbits, pullets and turkeys fall very much short
> of ours. At the house where we ate in Paris our diet was
> regular, having every noon soup, afterwards a dish of boiled
> meat, mutton and beef with some other dishes either of
> broiled mutton, or a pie, or cold beef stuffed with bacon, and
> last of all a dessert. At night we always had roast beef, or
> mutton, or veal with a salad, and also roasted fowls tame or
> wild larded for the most part with bacon, or else fricasseed;
> after this we never failed off a dessert.
> —Beinecke Rare Book and Manuscript Library,
> Yale University, Osborn Ms. B 155

undertaken in the pursuit of knowledge: the Paris Observatory
– established in 1667 and completed in 1671, though it would be
extended later – was the site of Jean-Dominique Cassini's work
on the eclipse times of Jupiter's satellites, which made possible the
prediction of eclipses and thus the calculation of longitude on land,
a technique developed by Galileo. The knowledge gleaned from

PARIS • A SHORT HISTORY

this work would be important to the formulation of Newton's theory of universal gravitation. Cassini's *Planisphere terrestre*, laid out in the Observatory to coordinate the astronomical information coming in from his correspondents, was affected by wear and tear, but fortunately his son had already printed his sketch map version in 1696. Paris today may not strike the casual visitor as a centre of astronomy, but it once formed part of the city's vibrant intellectual life.

Science, however defined, could only achieve so much in the capital. When the city was threatened by drought in 1696, the reliquary of Saint Geneviève was carried in procession. Again in 1725, the reliquary was paraded in the hope of stopping heavy rainfall before it led to flooding and a bad harvest. From 1731, rumours of miracle cures taking place at a tomb in the cemetery of the parish of Saint-Médard led to great interest (as discussed in Chapter 6).

Foreign visitors of this period generally spent much more time in Paris than in any other part of France. In Paris they saw a cityscape impressive in its power, activity, order and style. As with travellers to London, they focused not on the distant past – not on Notre-Dame and other buildings from the medieval period – but on works more recently constructed, such as Versailles and the Invalides. Their response to older buildings was generally unfavourable.

There was also an interest in new gardens, such as the one designed by André Le Nôtre at the château of Sceaux, a seat of Louis-Auguste, Duke of Maine, one of Louis XIV's bastards who was legitimized. John, Viscount Perceval wrote of:

> ...the fine prospect from the garden on every side, the great variety of walks and parterres, the fine canal and basin in which they often sail, a yacht lying always there at anchor, the particular good taste that appears in the disposition of the whole, and the neat order kept in all the parts.

Costs for tourists

FRANCES, DOWAGER COUNTESS OF SALISBURY, WIDOW OF THE 4TH
Earl, stayed in Paris in 1699 and 1702 with a large establishment.
A sample item, in livres and sols, from a bundle of their 'Weekly
expenses at Paris' includes the following:

	Sols		*Sols*
butcher	–	herbs and onions	12
fowls	6	10½ lb sugar	8
bread and flour	17	fruit	11
2 tongues	4	vinegar	4
2 lb bacon	4	oil	12
milk and cream	19	salads	4
11 lb butter	10	beans	6
fish	1	peas	5
artichokes	16	oranges	6
melons	–		

—From the Cecil papers held at Hatfield House, Hatfield,
Hertfordshire

The cost structure of tourism was very different to that of
today, if only because visits generally lasted for much longer.
Allowances were often expressed in terms of so much per month
or even year, and tourists when they arrived at Paris, intending
to stay for a while, tended to strike a bargain for a period
of weeks or months for their accommodation, and often for
their food.

Louis had purchased the property, originally built for his finance minister Jean-Baptiste Colbert, in 1699. It was confiscated during the Revolution, demolished and eventually, in the nineteenth century, replaced by a smaller château. That building is now the Musée de l'Île-de-France, one of many in the Paris area that deserve more appreciation today.

Paris for British visitors was the capital of a state that, under Louis XIV, appeared rather menacing, and the centre of a culture that could be disturbingly attractive. Italian cities such as Venice and Rome typically signified something different to travellers, including tourists; they were increasingly viewed as something akin to attractions in a modern-day theme park of the past. A common response to Paris, on the other hand (as would soon be the case in London too) was that it represented the modern world, a place that was moving away from archaic superstitions and challenging old beliefs, progressing towards the future.

Although tourists were fewer in number during Louis XIV's reign than today, their responses testified to the power of the French state and its focus on Paris. There was still a strong link between the ruling dynasty and the capital, a link that would be greatly tested in the eighteenth century and then abruptly severed. Yet it would be a mistake to think of eighteenth-century France only in terms of the imminent Revolution, or of Paris as a city dominated by anticipation of such an event. Instead, despite the food shortages and high prices that led to riots in 1725, it was largely characterized by an absence of serious trouble.

Chapter 6

An Age of Opulence, 1700–1750

Louis XIV's lengthy reign was followed, during the Regency of Philip, Duke of Orléans (1715–23), by an upsurge in intellectual speculation and cultural vitality. France had recently been defeated in the War of the Spanish Succession (1701–14), notably by the British under John, Duke of Marlborough, but it had also displayed considerable resilience and Paris had not been forced to surrender. Indeed, France was still regarded as a great power and centre of fashion, and this reputation provided a backdrop to its development as one of Europe's intellectual capitals. New talent was drawn to the city and new ideas became fashionable.

The period up to the 1760s saw the so-called *philosophes* grow in influence through Voltaire's popularization of Newton in the 1730s, Diderot's deistic works of the 1740s, and his *Encyclopédie*, launched in Paris in 1751, which became a means of disseminating advanced ideas to the educated public. The *Encyclopédie* very much reflected the values of the *philosophes* and those of Paris as a whole in that it was published in French, not Latin, and produced by subscription and individual support rather than by government commission. The particular intensity of the French Enlightenment owed much to the prominence of the public sphere, the consequent need to appeal for public support and the possibility of doing so. As a result, writers in effect called a public into existence, defined it, and helped ensure that it became a force in politics, or at least an idea to which appeals could be made.

Not all topics of discussion in the city, however, matched these intellectual heights. Robert Trevor, an early-career British diplomat, reported in 1729:

> There is an unphilosophical story of a woman brought to bed the other day at Paris of two young lions after having been to see a lion baited; that is believed at court, and generally through all France, and will probably make as great a noise as our rabbits.

He was referring to the equally bizarre news from England that a Godalming woman called Mary Toft had apparently given birth to rabbits.

A 1739 map of Paris by Louis Bretez, which is shown in this chapter, was known as the Turgot Plan after the city's effective mayor, Michel-Étienne Turgot, who had decided to promote Paris by commissioning the greatest example of urban cartography yet produced. The detailed measurements required for its preparation began in 1734 and took two years to complete. With an axonometric projection, oriented towards the south-east, the countryside sits close, although much nearby to Paris is divided into gardens. There are numerous boats on the river and the scale of 1:400 allows for an extraordinary amount of detail. Paris appears tidy and orderly, but as with other such maps, the effect is an illusion: the ever-present problems of city life continued. In 1737, Margaret, Viscountess Coningsby wrote to reassure her sister about difficulties with the water supply:

> I beg you'll be in no frights about the Seine water for we have it
> all passed through a sand fountain, which takes off the violent
> effects of it….I seldom drink it without wine and if it should
> disagree with me I would drink spa [mineral] water.

Turgot would also be responsible for commissioning the
Fontaine des Quatre-Saisons on the Rue de Grenelle (1739–45),
which was intended to address such problems on that part of the
Left Bank.

Public appreciation of art was on the rise, owing in part to the
exhibition of pictures in the Place Dauphine on Corpus Christi Day
and, more significantly, the public exhibitions held in the Salon
Carré of the Louvre (1667, 1673, 1699, 1704 and 1725; regularized
in 1737, and then held either annually or biennially). Known simply
as 'the salons', these exhibitions were controlled by the Académie
Royale de Peinture et de Sculpture, whose members enjoyed the
sole right to submit their work. The salons offered the public
an opportunity to view significant works of art and encouraged
the development of artistic criticism, which was to become an
important element of fashionable life as the idea of public taste
developed. Salon criticism began in 1747, when Étienne La Font
de Saint-Yenne published his thoughts on the 1746 Salon. At the
same time, the role of aristocrats as patrons and leaders of fashion
remained significant in Paris, even more so than in London –
most of the theatre posters displayed in Paris were found in the
aristocratic districts.

It was not only art that was discussed and criticized. Police
reports captured a vibrant public commentary on everything that
went on in the city and reflected governmental concerns. On 28
May 1733, for example, a police spy reported a rumour going
around Paris that Cardinal Fleury, the leading minister, did not

wish to see Louis XV fight in the developing international crisis over the succession to the Polish crown, preferring that he hunt; and that France had fallen from her seventeenth-century heights of grandeur and power.

There had, as this suggests, been an upsurge in political tension in 1730–2. In 1731, Louis XV replied to remonstrances from the *parlement* of Paris by characterizing it as simply an instrument by which the monarch made known his orders. He annulled a number of parliamentary decrees on ecclesiastical issues and in response, Parisian judges went on strike. Louis refused to grant an audience to hear the grievances of the *parlement* and in 1732 he had many of those involved expelled from the city.

The crisis quickly blew over; it was resolved by the end of the year, when the exiles were allowed to return. But its root cause, which was really ecclesiastical rather than constitutional, emphasizes the significance of religion to the history of Paris. Many of the *parlement*'s leading speakers at this time were inspired by religious fervour. Several had been sighted visiting the tomb of a Jansenist deacon in the cemetery of the Church of Saint-Médard, which local rumour had recently identified as the site of 'miraculous' cures. The cemetery became thronged with visitors, many of them praying and experiencing convulsions, claiming to be inspired by the Holy Spirit; others came along simply to watch what was happening. Eventually the phenomenon caused so much disruption that the cemetery had to be closed. It can, however, be visited today – it is located at the foot of the Rue Mouffetard, where the local market and the Square Saint-Médard attract tourists who know nothing of this eccentric episode in its history.

As political tensions eased after the crisis of 1732, the *parlement* condemned the *Judicium Francorum* to be burnt – this was a revised version of a radical pamphlet that had originally appeared during the *Fronde*, claiming that the *parlement* represented the nation. Additionally, the remonstrances against the levying of a wartime tax were relatively moderate in tone.

Although the amount of ambitious and costly building work going on in Paris at this time suggested a certain confidence in the future, there was much insecurity among Parisians at the individual level, particularly the poor. A famine in 1709 had led to many deaths and to criticism of the king, prompting calls for a government based upon Christian ideals with the king as an effective father of his people. Decades later, these concerns were still in the air. In the late 1740s there was an official push to eliminate the city's vagrant population; a proclamation was issued in the king's name, and the authorities began rounding people up and installing them in workhouses or other institutions. It subsequently emerged that some of those seized as vagrants had been sent to French Guiana (where many died after exposure to tropical diseases), with their captors being paid a bounty – and that a proportion of them were actually outside the scope of the proclamation. The following year saw the detention of children in Paris in another misguided effort to control the poor, leading to further outrage and rioting.

At a different level of care and its failings, the administration for veterans of the Hôtel des Invalides displayed paternalism, favouritism and the effects of social privilege, all of which were characteristic of both city and country. Reforms and financial expedients were inconsistently applied, and occasional royal visits and the distribution of largesse could not satisfy the needs of impoverished veterans. More traditionally, care was provided from, and in, the city's many clerical institutions.

Paris drew on the resources of the rest of the country by means of taxation, revenues and rents. It was also the centre of a supply system that covered much of France, providing demand but also extracting resources in periods of shortage. Lean cattle were driven from Auvergne to lush lower Normandy for fattening before being moved to the Parisian market; their slaughter and process-ing produced much of the city's waste, with the tanning processes involved in the production of leather a particular source of pollu-tion, much of which ended up in the Seine. Wine from all across France, notably Languedoc (red) and Anjou (white), served the city, while olive oil and fruit from southern France were moved via the Rhône and then overland before being taken by river and canal to Paris.

Tourists visited the city as a centre of civilization, polite society and the arts, and the leading European court. Although it did not possess the antiquities of Rome, the sensual allure of Venice, the art of Florence, or an opera house to compare with that of Naples, Paris boasted an enormous range of cultural and social activities in which visitors could participate; it had an active artistic life, many splendid sights and a dramatic royal court at nearby Versailles (see plate VII). Its proximity to Britain naturally made it a favoured destination of British visitors: Paris could be reached from Dover in three days, and there was no need to consider crossing the Alps to get there. Furthermore, unlike the great Italian cities, its climate was acceptable to the British all year long – and there was no equivalent to the malarial Pontine marshes near Rome. Many letters and diaries written by eighteenth-century British visitors have been preserved, providing a lively and accessible record of their impressions and experiences of Parisian life.

Thanks to the vitality of Paris, there was enough going on to interest tourists all year round – there was no need to rely on the presence of a court to guarantee a social life, as was the case in many other European cities. That said, the presence of the French court did have an impact on tourism. Visiting Versailles to watch the king take part in public rituals, particularly eating, attending mass, and hunting, was a popular pastime. A small number of tourists could be expected to receive entertainment at the highest social level, a process eased by the interaction and intermarriage of aristocratic elites. In 1715 Lord Harold, heir to the Duke of Kent, was introduced to Louis XIV, supped with the Duke of Noailles, met the Duke of Orléans, and found the Duke of Villeroi very civil; in August 1729, Marshal Villars, a leading councillor, entertained to dinner the Duke and Duchess of Richmond and the Duke of Hamilton. In 1736, the Marquis de Stainville, the Lorraine envoy in Paris, entertained Evelyn, 2nd Duke of Kingston and George, 3rd Earl of Cholmondeley 'with several other English gentlemen of distinction'. Such introductions were invaluable for establishing one's presence on the social scene.

For the rest of the tourist population, the city had a large range of accommodation available. Food was plentiful and generally of high quality. French was the foreign language most British tourists were conversant with, and the city was well used to dealing with them. The luxury trades, particularly tailoring, were a major attraction; Edmund Dewes, a servant, noted on the day after his arrival in 1773: 'Tailors, barbers, cutlers, merchants, all coming bowing, scraping to offer their services to my master in case he should want in their way: master now has got a footman, who comes in his bag and ruffles hanging on his finger ends.'

Tourists tended to spend a lot on clothes, largely because French fashions for men were quite different from those in Britain. On arrival in the city they realized they needed new clothes, and were typically beset by tailors. Charles Spencer apologized in 1723 to his grandmother, Sarah, Duchess of Marlborough – a stern overseer – for buying fine clothes in Paris, while in 1775 the young tourist Robert Wharton purchased new silk stockings and a pair of shoes, and was pleased at the low costs charged for laundry. Between 20 December 1749 and 17 May 1750, Sir John Swinburne spent 216 livres for a waistcoat of rich Lyons stuff, 84 for six pairs of worked ruffles, 1,367 for 'my taylor's bill', 299 for a lined crimson velvet coat and breeches, and 848 for the embroidering of 'a suit of cloaths in gold'; in 1751, he spent 210 livres on embroidering another suit, 60 on a laced hat and feather, and 719 on his tailor's bill. Such costs contributed to the expense of visiting Paris. In 1788 James Brogden, a future MP, wrote to his father: 'I fear I must forewarn you that my expenses at Paris by the accounts I every day hear of from travellers will much exceed my former, however extravagant you may have considered them.'

The principal tourist sights included the palaces – the Louvre, Tuileries, Luxembourg and the Duke of Orléans' Palais-Royal; the *hôtels* or townhouses of prominent residents; public buildings, especially the Invalides and the Observatory; squares, such as the Place des Victoires; luxury factories, particularly the Gobelins manufactory and the Sèvres porcelain factory; and, of course, churches such as Notre-Dame, Val-de-Grâce and Saint-Sulpice. In 1742, George, Viscount Beauchamp wrote to his father, Algernon, Earl of Hertford, answering a string of queries:

I think the air is rather sharper here than in England, but it is almost impossible to judge in so large a town and so full of smoke....The Louvre is the largest modern building I have seen here. It runs down a great way upon the side of the Seine and makes a great show.

I was the other morning in the Tuileries which is a charming garden. When you first enter there is a large open space with gravel walks and between the walks mince pie borders and in the middle a basin, but those borders are more to be excused because they have no turf that is fine enough for lawns.

Beauchamp bought clothes, sat for his portrait by Pattier, visited the theatre – seeing Molière's *Tartuffe* and Voltaire's *L'Enfant prodigue* – and saw the sights: the Gobelins works, the Invalides and Versailles, writing of the last: 'the Grand Apartments which really are not very grand, but furnished with tapestry, and some good pictures though nothing so fine as one might expect at the court of so vain a people'. In 1725, John, Lord Perceval focused on the major sights he and his wife Catherine had seen:

> We have seen the Invalides with their beautiful church, the Place des Victoires, the Theaters, the Palais or Parliament house, the Church of Notre Dame with the beautiful marble altar of Christ dead in his mother's lap, and the carved seats of the canons. Cardinal Noailles officiated that day being the great festival of the Virgin's nativity. We observed the whole service which consisted of much music and mummery, and we thought the Cardinal had at least as much reverence paid him, by kneeling, kissing his hand, incensing him etc. during the service, as either Christ or the Virgin.

Many tourists were also attracted by humbler scenes such as the open-air shows along the boulevards. In 1764, the attorney Thomas Greene and the painter George Romney viewed the outside of the Louvre:

> ...and were well entertained there by a mountebank and his monkey. We could not but admire the sagacity and drollery of the animal and at the same time could not forbear concluding that it

had much more the appearance of the human species than many strutting Frenchmen that we had seen.

This disparaging attitude was also captured in visual accounts such as *View on the Pont Neuf at Paris* (1771) by Henry Bunbury: the malnourished and therefore thin French depicted were a dog barber, lemonade seller, chocolate seller, sentry, lawyer, postilion, shoe cleaner and barber. They were shown as either foppish or beggarly, and their fashions were satirized in the use of muffs and a parasol. Only the porteress was plump.

Apart from Versailles, popular day trips by hired carriage included Saint-Germain-en-Laye, Saint-Cloud, Saint-Denis, Marly and Sceaux. Dr Edward Thomas travelled on a number of excursions in 1750, and his critical remarks are an instructive reminder that tastes changed and that many palaces were not well preserved.

> St. Cloud commands a charming prospect of Paris....A bad staircase of two flights of 27 steps each without a landing place and heavy marble. The gallery very fine but too much gilding but all going to decay. A most magnificent cascade in the gardens, and a water spout 130 foot high.

Versailles impressed him more, although it was the gardens that he particularly liked:

> This vast palace is situated on a rising ground beautifully sloping every way in the middle of a vast amphitheatre. The woods all around rising on the sides of the hills at an equal distance except where the two ground vistas are, one in front to Paris, and the back one through the gardens; and from the open arcade that leads to the gardens you have the grand canal full in view as well

as several basins, and beyond that an unbounded prospect through
an immense avenue. One is amazed to see the vast profusion of
white marble here, since all the stairs and edgings of the ponds
are of it. Besides the infinite number of statues. But there is much
regularity in these gardens. The orangery a stupendous work.

For Thomas and other tourists, the activities of the court helped
make the trip more interesting: it was a living palace. He visited
Versailles while Louis XV was in residence:

> I stayed a whole day at Versailles and saw the whole court in its
> grandeur. In the morning at ten all the courtiers were assembled
> in the Grand Gallery, soon after the King passed through it to
> the chapel, and on his entrance the band of music both vocal and
> instrumental began to play which continued the whole time he
> was at chapel which was but short, and it was impossible he could
> hear one word the priest said. After twelve the Queen, Dauphin,
> and the daughter went to chapel, and I saw her Majesty dine
> with little ceremony. Every female was painted except the Queen.
> The daughters were swarthy girls but have full black eyes. The
> Dauphin tall and fat.

Description was made more necessary by the absence of photogra-
phy in the eighteenth century. James Brogden saw Louis XVI and
Marie Antoinette (see plate IX) in 1788:

> I have been [to Versailles] to stare with the citizens at the Grand
> Monarch. I saw him and the Queen [Marie Antoinette] at mass
> and at dinner. He seemed to like the last of these entertainments
> much the best, at least if one may judge by the degree of attention
> which he paid to it in comparison to the first. I never saw such

a mockery of religion as this ceremony. In the first place I must inform you that the order of the chapel is kept by a company of soldiers with their muskets. The king upon his entrance is saluted by a flourish of drums – the service is very short, and had I not been told it was mass I should have thought it a concert of music. However the King and his two brothers seemed to pay very little attention to it being laughing and talking together the whole time without so much as opening their prayer books….the Queen is a prodigious fine woman carrying in her countenance the marks of ability. I was close to the table at which they dined and had a fine stare for half an hour.

Closer to the city, tourists walked or rode into the countryside to nearby villages.

Aside from the sights, Paris was fascinating because of the range of activities it could cater for. John Mitford wrote in 1777: 'Paris is always gay. In the winter it has only the gaieties of a town. In summer it has some of those of the country. Operas, plays, balls, and entertainments of various kinds, are perpetual resources for the idle.' Culture was readily available and Robert Wharton wrote of the theatres in 1775 that 'there is no mobbing. They dare not be noisy for there are soldiers ready to arrest the troublesome person. They may appear a mark of despotism but it is yet comfortable to the peaceable spectators.' In 1788, Brogden found the city

very gay, four play houses open every night and the opera three times a week….I should imagine myself in another London were it not the language was different, the same bustle of carriages, the same throng of people, the streets to be sure are not so broad as the streets of London but they are neither so narrow nor so dirty as we English are apt from prejudice to suppose them.

Interests, hobbies and vices could all be pursued in an attractive setting and the activities of British visitors varied greatly. In 1722 the British envoy was asked to help one Dr Charles Bale, who visited 'with the design of seeing the practice of midwifery in the Hôtel-Dieu'. John, later 2nd Earl of Egmont, travelled to Paris in 1726 with his father, who described him as growing 'very fond of antiques…bought a great many glass seals, copies of the French King's collection, which he proposes to place in a cabinet, this is the beginning of virtuosoship'.

French food and the guidebook

FRENCH FOOD HAS A REPUTATION FOR EXCELLENCE, BUT IT HAS NOT always been as strong as it was from the late nineteenth century to the late twentieth. Indeed, there has recently been a decline in this reputation, making critical earlier comments of interest.

From the anonymous *Gentleman's Guide in his Tour Through France*. By an Officer who lately travelled on a principle which he most sincerely recommends to his countrymen, viz., not to spend more money in the country of our national enemy than is required to support with decency the character of an Englishman (7th edition, 1783):

> The French certainly do not eat so great a quantity of solid meat as the English; nor do they dress it in the same manner; soup, fricassees, hashes, and ragouts, are preferred before whole joints, boiled or roasted; they choose to keep their meat so long before it is dressed, that it is so very tender, and stinks so frequently, that an unfrenchified Englishman is sure to be often disappointed at his meals.

Conversely, the actor David Garrick recorded of one of his days in Paris: 'Did very little this day but idle and eat and drink.' On 18 September 1725, *Mist's Weekly Journal*, the leading London Tory newspaper, recounted how British tourists in Paris would go drinking until two or three in the morning, 'then return home, unless they chance to stumble into a bordel [brothel] by the way; a misfortune which has often happened...the whole account of their travels is generally no more than a journal of how many bottles they have drunk, and what loose amours they have had'. On 7 August 1731, 'Civicus', in an attack on travel in the *London Journal*, stressed the sexual risks presented by women travelling: 'it is highly probable, that by means of our ladies travelling, some of our noble families may be honoured with a French dancing master's son for their heirs'. There was a clear sexual allusion in a newspaper comment of 1739: 'I look upon France as the hot-bed to our English youth, where they are immaturely ripened, and therefore soon become rotten and corrupt at home.'

According to one London newspaper, Paris was 'a city the most noted for intrigues of any in Europe'. Access to local society was relatively easy for visitors, and there were numerous sex workers. Sexual conquests were of great interest to the press:

> Our gentry will make themselves as famous in making conquests among the French women, as their brave ancestors have been heretofore in subduing the French men....We hear from Paris, that one of the dancers at the Opera, called La Salle, so remarkable for her chastity, as to have obtained the name of Vestal, has at last surrendered to a young English nobleman, who was introduced to her at an assembly in woman's apparel, and so far insinuated himself into her favour as to be permitted to take part of her bed.

Thomas, 2nd Viscount Weymouth caused diplomatic complica-
tions when he took his mistress, Mlle Petit Pas, back to Britain in
1732. She was a leading dancer at the Opéra and, 'being of the
French King's music, and consequently a menial servant of His
Majesty's she ought to be sent back'. Petit Pas indeed returned to
Paris in May 1733 'avec quarante mille livres, beaucoup de joie, et
un petit milord dans le ventre'. A pamphlet, *Letter to a Celebrated
Young Nobleman on his late Nuptials* (1777), fancifully depicted the
prior conduct of Charles, 2nd Viscount Maynard: 'those amiable
days when you were drawn gently along the Boulevards at Paris,
reclined in the arms of an Opera dancer, who was supporting
your pallid figure'. Some travellers treated the theatres primarily as places to pick up women. According to the travel writer
Philip Thicknesse:

> It is certain that men of large fortunes can in no city in the world
> indulge their passions in every respect more amply than in Paris;
> and that is the lure which decoys such numbers, and in particu-
> lar Englishmen, to this city of love and folly; and occasions such
> immense sums to be drained from other countries, and lavished
> away in debauchery of every kind, in a town infinitely inferior to
> London. I verily believe Paris to be the theatre of more vice than
> any city in the world, drunkenness excepted.

Thicknesse claimed that even devout Parisian wives were generous with their sexual favours. He was sardonic about the sexual
adventures of British tourists, writing about a gift of £1,000 from
the son of an English duke

> to one little piece of ready-made love....This is one instance, and
> I could give you a thousand of the great influence of novelty,

change of country, and of manners; for in London the same woman, and consequently the same charms, would not have produced a tythe [tenth] of such liberality. But it was Paris, a Paris Opera girl, and an Englishman at Paris, who is nobody without he cuts a figure.

Given that many tourists would have had access to the sex workers of London as well as other opportunities for relations with women, it is worth considering why Parisian women proved so attractive. It is possible that much of their appeal lay in the element of unfamiliarity. Lord Dalrymple, brother of the British envoy, was not especially impressed by the women in 1715:

I have not been long enough here to know whether London or Paris is the most diverting town. The people here are more gay, the ladies less handsome, and much more painted, love gallantry, more than pleasure, and coquetry more than solid love. This place is good for all those, that have more vanity than real lust....This is the most diverting time to be at Paris because of the Fair Saint Germain. All the ladies go there every night at six o'clock and stay till then. All that time they stroll about from the fair to the play and rope dancing and the rest of the things to be seen there and I am sure if the people there have a mind to be happy there is no difficulty to lose themselves. It is impossible to take more freedom than that place allows of, and men and women stroll about without ceremony....My brother being here makes it easy for me to get into good company though I am not as yet in love with anybody nor are the ladies handsome. I believe I shall only make love as I used to do to some chambermaid. I have already had some adventures of that kind.

Beauchamp thought Parisian women unattractive:

> I have seen but one pretty woman and she was a Dutch woman.
> But they are so cheerful and polite that they are very agreeable.
> It is impossible to know what the ladies are[,] for though they
> are extremely well dressed (that is genteely for they are always
> dirty) they smear themselves so with paint that it is quite a
> ridiculous sight.

In 1755, however, Lord Nuneham confessed to his sister that he
found French fashions alluring: 'I never could nor never shall bear
anything but the French dress for ladies, and I am fonder of rouge
well put on than ever…to me the finest pale face, the finest shape
ill dressed is nothing.'

The sexual appeal of France was multifaceted. First, it was on
offer. John Jervis, later an admiral victorious over the French, noted
of his time in Paris in 1772: 'afterwards to the Tuileries gardens
and walked by moonlight, which would have been extremely
agreeable, but for the interruption of too many of the votaries of
Venus for the most part of the lowest class'. Philip Francis noted
another dimension, the allure of French sexuality: 'In England
the commerce between the sexes is either passion or pleasure; in
France it is gallantry, sentiment or intrigue; in Italy it is a dull
insipid business.' Archibald Macdonald in 1764, spending most
of his time in Paris, reported:

> A French woman knows well enough that a stranger is a bird
> of passage and that she has no firm hold of him, whereas she
> can make one of her own countrymen her humble servant, and
> commonly knows where to give the preference.…I have kept
> a snug piece these six months whom I visit every day and who

comforts me amply for the cruelties of the ladies.....Marriages are formed here by the parents without the parties ever having seen each other.... You therefore see every day men living with married women who are not their wives, and wives living with married men who are not their husbands without any kind of scandal or reproach.

There were, of course, also opportunities for male tourists to find male sexual partners. In 1717, George Carpenter

could not help observing one thing that was entirely new to me, which was several boys that walked about in the evenings to be picked up, as women do about the playhouses in London. The whores seemed to be very angry at this....I heard some of them say aloud that it had almost quite spoilt their trade.

Problems were created when impressionable young men fell in love. Venereal disease was bad, but so was a *mésalliance*. Tourists might become involved either with female British tourists, or with local women. There was a real risk that all this activity would upset the careful matrimonial economy of dowries and connections; it therefore represented a more serious threat to aristocratic prestige and parental supervision than other forms of tourist activity.

Gambling played a prominent role in polite French society. The British generally gambled a lot at home (to the despair of contemporary moralists), so it was not surprising that when they went to France many gambled heavily. People gambled on news and on sports, but most tourists gambled on cards. Edward Mellish wrote to his father in 1731, 'The French only regard strangers according to the money they spend and figure they make with their equipages, and provided you game and play you will be well received in the best company at Paris.' Visiting Paris the same year, Andrew Mitchell commented on the Parisian custom of gambling in respectable houses on the footing of an assembly, where the banker paid the lady of the house for the privilege of fleecing her guests: 'I know several gentlemen drawn in unwarily to such company, which obliged them to leave the place sooner than they otherways would have done.'

Comparisons with London were frequent. In 1727, William Freman observed:

> Paris is very handsome, not near so big as London, but the streets in general very much larger and abundantly better paved, it being a broad pavement about a six inch square, the lights are hung in the middle of the street by a string cross, which at night has a very pretty effect, especially the Tuilieries from the Pont Neuf.

Edmund Dewes noted in 1776 that Paris had 'something the appearance of London for hurry and bustle but much dirtier to walk the streets there being no particular parts for foot people to walk upon' – which was a frequent observation by tourists. It wasn't until the 1770s that a Parisian street, the Rue de l'Odéon, would have pavements with gutters. However, William Mildmay, a London lawyer, wrote in 1730:

> ...in regard to the clearness of air, pavement of streets, and number of great hotels [aristocratic houses], it is by far the finer, neater and more agreeable place: it is rather like a country town than a capital city, for from the very gates you enter into a wood on one side and into corn fields on the other; nor does one meet with that concourse of people as are always passing through

and from in and near London, so that it is as private and retired within one mile's distance, as within forty. The houses are for the most part built of stone, the country about abounding with quarries. The streets are narrow and consequently inconvenient for foot passengers, there not being room to fix up posts to protect them from the coaches. The squares or places are very beautiful, the houses being all built in one taste regularly answering to one another.…The private houses or hotels of the nobility and gentry are dispersed throughout in great numbers: for almost every person of fortune in France has here a house of his own, in which he makes his constant residence; on the contrary but few English gentlemen think themselves at home in London, choosing to live (or at least they did formerly) upon their own estates in the country. And this it is that makes Paris so much more beautiful – than London; at the same time the chief of this beauty does not appear in the architecture without, but rather in the richness and elegancy of the furniture within, though in some place the too great profusion of looking glass and painting, the darling taste of the French, renders those apartments rather tawdry than noble.

As previously mentioned, the development in the western suburbs under the Regency and thereafter owed much to the proximity of the royal court at Versailles, a situation comparable to the development in what became London's West End. The role of entrepreneurial landowners was less to the fore in Paris than in London, and the emphasis was less on residential squares. Instead, Princes of the [royal] Blood had what were in effect courts of their own, which included architects and artists; for instance, Jean Aubert, court architect of the Bourbon-Condé family, helped to build the Bourbon palace in Paris (1724–9).

British tourists developed their responses to the city in part by discussing with each other their impressions of what they had seen, often while congregating in cafés and restaurants. In 1732, a police spy noted that many English were usually at a café in the Rue Dauphine, a street in Saint-Germain-des-Prés in the 6th arrondissement. In 1788, James Buller went to the Café Conti, also on Rue Dauphine, to read the English papers.

It was possible to lodge with private individuals (Sir John Blair did so in 1787 in order to learn French), but most tourists stayed in hotels. 'They all generally lodge in the Fauxbourg S. Germain,' noted the *Daily Post-Boy* of 27 September 1731. The Hôtel de l'Impératrice in the Rue Jacob, a popular destination, was reportedly comfortable; one tourist reported, 'we have an elegant dining room, with two bed chambers on the first floor, and a bed chamber in the entresol, with an apartment for the servant, for three guineas per week. I confess the lodgings are dear, but the situation is good, and the furniture magnificent.' Others were less satisfied. Jane Parminter stayed at the Hôtel de la Ville de Rome in 1785: 'a very dirty inn indeed, the staircase shaking, the maids bold and impertinent, the treatment sparing and the charge extravagant'. Several travellers wrote of being pestered by bugs.

In his 1753 play *The Englishman in Paris*, Samuel Foote has his character Squire Buck remark of an English resident in the city: 'The rascal looks as if he had not had a piece of beef and pudding in his paunch these twenty years; I'll be hanged if the rogue has not been fed upon frogs ever since he came over.' Roast beef served to define the superior quality of their native cuisine for many tourists. In Paris in 1764, Thomas Greene 'saw with inexpressible pleasure, what I had not seen for six weeks, a large piece of roasted beef'.

British tourists could be difficult. In 1723 the young and lively John Lindsay, 20th Earl of Crawford, threw a French marquis who was rude to him into a pond at Versailles; a few years later, a group of Britons caused a scene on Christmas night by blocking a passage outside the Cordelier's church. They also occasionally ran into problems with other British people they encountered abroad. In 1714, Charles, 1st Duke of Richmond was attacked on the Pont Neuf because he had offended a member of the Jacobite court at Saint-Germain-en-Laye:

> Richard Hamilton…resented some disrespectful words spoken by his Grace against that court in an assemblée in his presence, who taking two or three friends with him to secure the footmen, forced the Duke out of his coach, and, after much threatening to beat him if he would not draw, he gave him two wounds.

As well as being Europe's leading destination for tourists Paris was a major producer of luxury goods, and it became the centre of the European art trade during the first half of the eighteenth century. Foreign rulers such as Elector Max Emanuel of Bavaria (*r.* 1662–1726) made large-scale purchases of French artworks, and from 1748 Duke Karl Eugen of Württemberg retained a Parisian agent whose only task was to supply all new French publications, court circulars and manuals of architecture and decorative style. James, Earl Waldegrave, envoy in 1730–40, was asked to source the best cook in France, burgundy, truffles and a Périgord pie for his boss, Thomas, Duke of Newcastle, Secretary of State for the Southern Department, as well as the very fine feather brushes used for cleaning the gilding of rooms for another connection, Lady Katherine Pelham. Waldegrave's predecessor, Stephen Poyntz, had also sent truffles, pâté and other delicacies regularly to Newcastle. The detailed records of such activities, suggestive as they are of sensual appreciation and indulgence, might not seem to match the backdrop of dignified, orderly classical-style buildings against which they played out at the centre of one of the world's more far-flung empires – but then, the contrast between mannered order and individualistic exuberance has always been part of Paris's history.

Chapter 7

Towards Revolution, 1750–1789

In the second half of the eighteenth century, Paris became more magnificent than ever as major public works provided the city with axial points of movement and interest. The nearest comparison was with the baroque rebuilding of parts of Rome by Sixtus V (r. 1585–90) and his successors. Work began on the Place Louis XV – now the Place de la Concorde – in 1755 and continued until 1775, while the Pont de la Concorde was built in 1788–90. Although London also acquired new bridges in this period, as well as squares in the new residential areas of the West End, none of these squares were comparable to the Place Louis XV.

In 1758, on the highest point of the Left Bank, work began on the Church of Sainte-Geneviève that would eventually become the Panthéon; and in 1763 Louis XV laid the first stone for the Church of Sainte-Marie-Madeleine, better known as the Madeleine, near a thirteenth-century church that was too small for this developing neighbourhood and would be demolished in 1901. The new church, however, was still incomplete when the Revolution came. Churches themselves changed in 1776 when a royal decree made it harder to be buried within them, a step intended to improve health. There was also concern for health reasons about city centre churchyards, such as the very large Cemetery of the Holy Innocents; these were regarded as a source of deadly vapours.

Tourists came in increasing numbers after the Seven Years' War with Britain ended in 1763, a process eased by the cessation of French support for the Jacobite claim to the British throne. Two years later, Elizabeth, second daughter of the 4th Earl of Berkeley, in Paris with her mother and sister, referred to 'the young Englishmen that swarmed about us'. James, 2nd Earl of Fife, spent more than £1,700 in the course of a few weeks during a visit in the winter of 1766–7 – but he was accompanied by his wife, 'lived in the first company in Paris', and spent much on clothes as well as on china, furniture, tapestries and damasks for his London house. The cost of Paris life led to James, later 7th Earl of Salisbury, receiving an additional £400 in 1770 on top of his monthly allowance; but five years later, a tourist with more modest tastes wrote home: 'I think one might live very comfortably from £300 a year or with a little management of £250.' This was the century that saw the rise of the restaurant, and in 1787 John Mitford claimed that supper and accommodation in Paris cost him at least six times as much as in Brussels. Paris had an intimidating reputation, and fear of the expense clearly led some tourists to change their plans.

The written accounts of British visitors continued to reflect various low-level clashes of culture and expectations. Care provided by Parisian doctors was often deemed unsatisfactory, as noted by the Countess Spencer in 1767 after she had colic:

> I have been forced to submit to the manners of the place and I have been squirted with clysters almost incessantly which have at last relieved me a little. Madame de Guerchi is my physician and really does very well if she did not tell the whole circle of men, how often I have a motion and how many more lavements I am to

LE PLAN DE PARIS, SES FAUBOURGS et SES ENVIRONS,
Meridiens et Paralleles par Minutes et Secondes. Gravé par MATTHIEU SEUTTE

Monceaux

LES
PORCHERONS

FAUB DE
RICHELIEU

LE ROULE

Marais de la Ville
l'Evêque

FAUBOURG
St. HONORÉ

les Champs Elysées

LA R. DE SEINE

le Pt aux Chevaux

FAUBOURG G

SEINE R

St.

GERMAIN

Plaine
de
Grenelle

FAUB St.

MICHEL
Chartreux

Renvoy

A. Saint Jean le Rond
B. Saint Denis du Pas
C. Hôtel Dieu
D. Enfans Trouvés
E. Saint Chrystophe
F. Ste Geneviève des Ardans
G. Saint Pierre aux Boeufs
H. Sainte Marine
I. Saint Landry
K. Saint Denis de la Chartre
L. Saint Symphorien
M. Bureau de l'Hôtel Dieu
N. la Magdelaine
O. Sainte Croix
P. Saint Germain le Vieil
Q. Saint Martial
R. Saint Eloy, jus Bernabitus
S. Saint Bartolemy
T. Saint Pierre des Arcis
V. la Sainte Chapelle
X. Cour de la Moignon
Y. Rue de Jerusalem
Z. l'Orloge du Palais

Six cens pas Geometriques valant cinq cent Toises
1 2 3 4 5 6 7 8 9 10 11 12
Douze cens Pas Communs
un Quart de Lieue Commune de France

take with a long dissertation on how much more convenient their squirts are than our method of doing the same thing.

In 1786, faced with the illness of her mother while in Paris, Frances, Lady Crewe sent for one Dr Lee:

> an English physician, who had resided here since he left off practice, and is good enough to give assistance to people of our own country when they stand in need of it…a plain good sort of regular physician.…But, had he been the lowest in our school he would have been worthy fifty of the French practitioners who talk such old fashioned nonsense, even the best of them, about bleeding in the foot, a seventh day crisis, and a thousand other long exploded notions, as prove them to be very far behind us in this science. It is not likely indeed the case should be otherwise for the profession is treated in so humiliating a way that no gentleman can enter into it…in general they are certainly bunglers.

The future general Sir John Moore, visiting Paris in 1772 with his father, disliked the French fashion of dressing children like adults but

> could only express his displeasure by gestures. Mutual offence was taken, and the parties proceeded to hostilities; but as French boys know nothing of boxing, they were thrown to the ground one across the other.

In 1786, Frances Crewe encountered the rising disapproval of the pit when she hung her cloak over the front of the box during a performance of the burlesque play *Le Roi de Cocagne* in Paris: 'I have since thought their etiquettes are cruel in the case of strangers who can never learn them by such experiences as mine.' Somewhat differently that year, she was stopped on the way to Versailles by:

> one of the horses tumbling down, and my maid and I being detained upon the bridge…three quarters of an hour, – both terrified to death, because we were on so narrow a part of it that every carriage which came by gave us a shock, as if it meant to tip us over into the Seine.

The scale of Paris's expansion during this period is shown on a map of the city and its principal buildings by Jacques Esnauts and Michel Rapilly, first published in 1784 and appearing in several significantly revised editions up to 1802. It is adorned with a masthead featuring a nymph of the Seine and an allegory of Paris with the symbols of the arts and sciences. Indexes in each margin identify important streets, parishes, colleges, hospitals, buildings, squares and other places of interest, which can be pinpointed by using letter and number references in the horizontal and vertical axes.

With the growth of the city in terms of both scale and development came changes in artistic and architectural style, notably the rise of neoclassicism, which can be seen in the treatment of ecclesiastical buildings. Jacques-Germain Soufflot's Church of Sainte-Geneviève, built between 1758 and 1790, had classical pillars; Thomas Brand observed: 'It is very fine – the Corinthian order shines in all its purity and just proportions. There are no buildings near it. It is seen to great advantage and does infinite honour to the taste of the architect.' Existing churches were also altered, typically by giving the bases and capitals of their pillars a classical look and by removing stained glass. Much Gothic ornamentalism, now judged hideous, was removed, including the altars, rood screens and choir stalls of Saint-Germain l'Auxerrois in 1756.

A night at the opera, 1785

ANTONIO SALIERI'S *LES DANAÏDES* (1784), WITH A FRENCH LIBRETTO, was first staged in Paris with great success. A British tourist, William Bennet, recorded his impressions of the production:

> The music loud and noisy in the French taste, and the
> singers screamed past all power of simile to represent. The
> scenery was very good, no people understanding the jeu de
> theatre or tricks of the stage so well as the French. We had
> in the dark scenes not above one light, and in the bright ones
> above twenty large chandeliers, so as to make a wonderful
> contrast, nor was there the least error or blunder in changing
> the scenes, except once when a candle pulled up too hastily,
> was very near setting fire to a whole grove of trees....Our
> opera ended with a representation of Hell in which the fifty
> Danaïdes were hauled and pulled about as if the devils had
> been going to ravish them, several of them in the violence
> of the action being literally thrown flat upon their backs;
> and they were all at last buried in such a shower of fire, that
> I wonder the playhouse was not burned to the ground.
> —Bodleian Library, Oxford, Ms. Eng. Misc. f. 54
> fols 174–5

The ongoing building and renovation of churches was a contrasting backdrop to some changes of a very different nature. By the 1760s, the intellectual style of the *philosophes* dominated in fashionable Parisian circles and the institutions of metropolitan culture were under their influence. However, their pretensions, real and supposed, offended many. In 1768, the young Genevan academic Horace Bénédict de Saussure wrote of the noted intellectual Jean-François Marmontel:

> I recognized in him what I had been warned to expect in Parisian *beaux esprits* – a very arbitrary tone, a habit of speaking of his set as the only one to be called philosophic, and of despising and making odious insinuations against those who did not belong to it.

Separately, there was on the part of some authorities a sense of concern about subversion, the *philosophes* being described to the *parlement* in 1759 by the Attorney General as 'a society organized… to destroy religion, to inspire a spirit of independence and to nourish the corruption of morals'.

In practice, most intellectual speculation had no such revolutionary intentions. For example, the Jardin du Roi – today the Jardin des Plantes, a pleasant site too rarely frequented by visitors – was the setting for a major project of intellectual achievement. Its influential director Georges-Louis Leclerc, Comte de Buffon, produced a 36-volume *Histoire naturelle* (1749–89) that achieved great popularity and fame, testifying to the fashion for encyclopaedic knowledge being organized as a means of enabling humanity to fulfil its potential – in this case, by replacing Carl Linnaeus's comprehensive system for the classification of animals and plants. Far from being a passive recipient of information, Buffon experimented, notably with crossbreeding, in order to use hybridity as an element in advancing a new definition of species that acknowledged both their constancy and their variation.

Publishers who produced sizeable multi-volume works, such as Charles-Joseph Panckoucke, had to be sensitive to the market, and the demands of the public also shaped other areas of cultural activity. Matching the activity of private patrons was an increasingly organized Parisian art market, which helped to heighten interest in French art.

Picture sales became more frequent, and attractively printed and compiled auction catalogues fostered interest. Sales at auctions for which a catalogue was printed rose from an annual average of three in the early 1750s to one of thirty for 1774–84. By the mid-1770s no fewer than sixty picture and print dealers were operating in Paris, and by the end of the 1780s there were four major salerooms. The ambience of these settings became more clearly commercial and impersonal. Whereas mid-eighteenth-century catalogues had often opened with a panegyric of the collector or a statement extolling the pleasures of collecting, later in the century the investment opportunities in buying paintings were presented more clearly. As with Diderot's *Encyclopédie*, the public, commercial character of culture was readily apparent.

Yet, rather than the public, there were *publics* – many of whom faced difficult immediate circumstances, not to mention uncertain futures. Even for the more fortunate, there was an uneasy sense of social menace that reflected some elements of the plight of the wider population. The shortage of available jobs in Paris did not prevent migration to the city, a consequence of the rising population and worsening conditions of life in the rural areas of the Paris basin. This contributed to a decline in real wages, the effect of which was exacerbated by price rises affecting rent, bread and firewood. Even water was an issue – there were more than 10,000 people for every public fountain. By the 1780s, as an indicator of social dysfunction, more than 650 children were being abandoned in the city every month.

Fears about widespread disorder led, from 1764, to a renewed emphasis on the incarceration of beggars and vagrants. This development was connected not only to the general increase in population and poverty but to the demobilization of soldiers after the Seven Years' War (1756–63), which had released adult men, habituated to violence and usually unskilled, into a labour market that was simply unable to absorb them.

Ballooning

PARIS WAS A KEY SITE IN THE DEVELOPMENT OF EARLY BALLOON flights as they worked up to carrying humans. In 1783, the first living beings – a sheep, a duck and a rooster – were flown by the Montgolfier brothers, using their realization that hot air could cause a balloon to rise. The animals, riding in a basket attached to a balloon, reached an altitude of about 1,500 feet in a display before Louis XVI at Versailles. Later that year, the first test flights with humans – initially tethered, and then flying free – took place in the Paris area.

Soon afterwards, the physicist Jacques Charles designed and flew a balloon in which the lifting agent was hydrogen, which it had been discovered was lighter than air. He rose to about 1,800 feet. In the 1790s, the French began to use balloons for reconnaissance in wartime.

As early as the 1750s, seditious comments often cited the high price of bread and the general misery of the people as reasons why Louis XV should be killed. These problems were not unique to France; Britain also saw riots over the price of bread. But there were various other tensions and sources of social pressure specific to Paris. Concerned in 1784 about the supply of firewood to the city, the *parlement* criticized the wood merchants responsible. Its opposition to what it considered their excessive profits was made clear – only for the government to reply that the best way to supply Paris was to enable its merchants to make a profit.

Alongside all of this, there were efforts to temper authority and power with justice. In Paris and the region under its *parlement*, death sentences were uncommon, and in the period 1735–89, one in four was commuted. At least seven magistrates had to concur before a severe punishment was imposed.

The increase in political tension had been modest until the early 1770s when a clash between government and *parlement* led to the exile of judges and an attempt to remodel the *parlement*, the defenders of which stressed its role in representing the people. The accession of a new king, Louis XVI, in 1774 brought with it a change of personnel and policy that helped resolve the crisis, and from that point until 1786 the *parlement* was more circumspect and docile than it had been for decades. Encouraged by success in the War of American Independence, in which France took part from 1778 to 1783, the tax increases of the early 1780s passed with ease.

There was no inevitability about the coming of revolution. The root cause was a lack of adequate royal leadership, exacerbated by a divided elite; the loss of prestige caused by failure in the international crisis of 1787, when France was faced down by Prussia and its ally Britain during a period of instability in the Dutch Republic, also played a part. None of that was unavoidable. The contrast in October 1789 between the delirious celebrations with Vienna's population greeted news of the capture of Belgrade, and the forced transfer to Paris of Louis XVI and his court after Parisians had invaded the palace of Versailles, is a reminder of the political value of success and the role of chance. The monarchy had also been tarnished by recent scandals, especially Marie Antoinette's (in fact totally innocent) involvement in the fraudulent Diamond Necklace Affair of 1784–6, a confidence trick involving a massive swindle. There had been comparable scandals during Louis XIV's reign – not least the 'Affair of the Poisons' in 1677–82 – yet he had not been at risk as an adult ruler. The loss of royal control in the Revolution, like the *Fronde* of 1648–53, showed that Paris had only changed so much in the intervening period.

Chapter 8

Revolution and Napoleon, 1789–1815

A revolution was about to launch in Paris that would wrack Europe and the Western world with conflict and instability – but in 1789 this seemed far from inevitable, as the Crown summoned an Estates-General in an effort to find a way out of serious financial difficulty. The political background was one of uncertainty, not incipient chaos. In 1788, James Buller wrote:

> ...took a long walk on the boulevards...saw the Bastille. Very strong buildings and the most dreadful place I ever could conceive. Almost hid from the town in every point of view, as if the people themselves were ashamed of a monument so disgraceful to humanity.

There was, in many circles, little sense of what was to come. On 14 May 1789, John, 3rd Duke of Dorset, the British ambassador – who had once let his mistress, the Italian ballerina Giovanna Baccelli, dance at the Opéra wearing his Order of the Garter – reported:

> All unquiet in the town, but the guards and patroles are as numerous as ever, reinforcements of troops are also arriving

every day, and the smallest disturbance is suppressed with an incredible activity.

Paris still had very few factories, so her revolutionary movements were not primarily the achievements of factory workers. However, the Réveillon riots that took place in April, centred on a small wallpaper factory of that name, were an important harbinger of later mob activity in the capital. (Jean-Baptiste Réveillon was a relatively benign employer and a major patron of the Montgolfier brothers. His factory and home were destroyed in the riots, in which twenty-five people were killed.) Only in the northern suburbs were there a few large textile manufactories employing between 400 and 800 workers. One-third of Parisian workers at this time were employed in the traditional building trade.

Much of the drama of the subsequent Revolution played out in the capital. This included the overthrow of royal authority, the violent seizure of the Bastille on 14 July (see plate XI) and the destruction of most of the customs posts around the city. Models of the Bastille can be viewed today at the Musée Carnavalet.

Louis's reluctance to accept reform continued to foster uncertainty and mistrust, and by October that year the ongoing bread shortages in the city led to fresh action. Rumours of preparations for a counter-revolution prompted a Parisian crowd, including many women, to march on Versailles on 5 October, determined to bring Louis to Paris. After the Queen's apartments were stormed by a section of the crowd the following day, Louis, under pressure, finally moved to the Tuileries Palace. With Versailles abandoned and the volatile metropolis ever more the centre of politics, royal authority and power were shattered. It was no surprise that the king tried to flee his capital in July 1791 for the safety of a frontier fortress from which he could negotiate the restoration of his

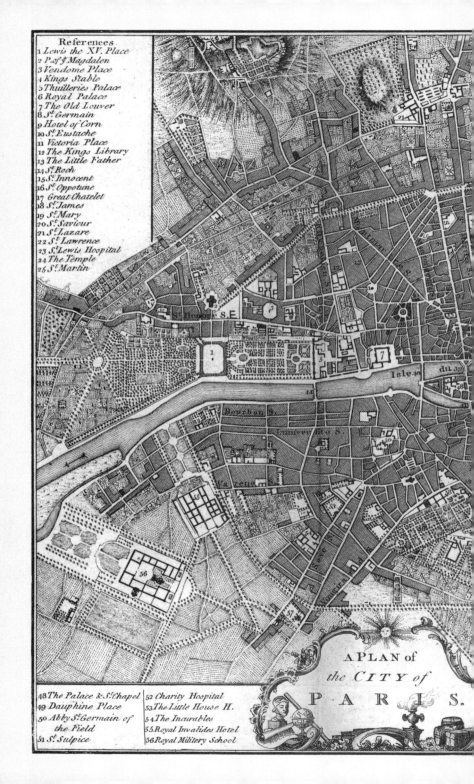

References.
1 Lewis the XV. Place
2 P. of S: Magdalen
3 Vendome Place
4 Kings Stable
5 Thuilleries Palace
6 Royal Palace
7 The Old Louver
8 S: Germain
9 Hotel of Corn
10 S: Eustache
11 Victoria Place
12 The Kings Library
13 The Little Father
14 S: Roch
15 S: Innocent
16 S: Oppotune
17 Great Chatelet
18 S: James
19 S: Mary
20 S: Saviour
21 S: Lazare
22 S: Lawrence
23 S: Lewis Hospital
24 The Temple
25 S: Martin

48 The Palace & S: Chapel
49 Dauphine Place
50 Abby S: Germain of
   the Field
51 S: Sulpice

52 Charity Hospital
53 The Little House H.
54 The Incurables
55 Royal Invalides Hotel
56 Royal Military School

A PLAN of
the CITY of
PARIS.

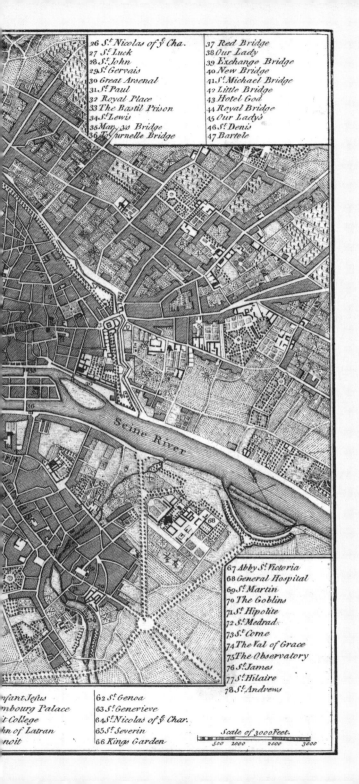

authority, only to be recognized, stopped by a crowd at Varennes, and returned to Paris.

Scenes of violence continued in the capital. In the storming of the Tuileries in August 1792, when the radicals seized power, the largely Swiss garrison was slaughtered. A British diplomatic messenger reported the mob 'industriously' disfiguring the faces of its victims 'by roasting them' in fires and carrying out an indiscriminate massacre without any regard for age or sex. Subsequently, on 2 and 3 September 1792, all but two of Paris's prisons – full of those arrested on suspicion of treason – were broken into and makeshift tribunals were erected. There were acquittals, but from 2 to 7 September 1,100 to 1,400 people were executed. Most were politically innocuous, many common criminals. Over 200 priests were killed in the course of these massacres, a consequence of the clergy's very close association with the Crown.

Paris was the site of all the Revolution's most significant public executions: Louis XVI and Marie Antoinette in 1793, followed by figures such as Georges Danton, Jacques Hébert and Maximilien Robespierre in 1794. They were all sent to the guillotine, which was regarded as an efficient and relatively humane way to end life – it had replaced breaking on the wheel and other harsh or inefficient practices. The guillotine was also used regardless of class. Most executions were carried out in the Place de la Révolution (formerly the Place Louis XV; now the Place de la Concorde). Louis XVI's body, with his head placed at his feet, was transported to the old church of La Madeleine and thrown into a pit of quicklime.

There were also large public ceremonies in Paris, such as the Festival of Unity and Indivisibility, which attracted massive crowds in 1793. At this event Hérault de Séchelles, president of the National Convention, paid tribute to the fecundity of nature, which was depicted as the centre of a religious cult of identity.

By February 1793 Britain and France were at war and tourism had ceased – in contrast to the excitement that had encouraged some daring would-be visitors from 1789 onwards, including William Wordsworth in 1792. One correspondent wrote in October 1789 of having seen soldiers' heads being carried about on spikes in the Tuileries. That summer, after the fall of the Bastille, Francis, Duke of Leeds, the Foreign Secretary, wrote to the ambassador:

> In the present distracted state of France, it is much to be wished that His Majesty's subjects should abstain from visiting that country as much as possible, and that they should not sacrifice to curiosity, either their own individual safety or the attention due to their character as British subjects. As however it is almost impossible that a considerable number of the King's subjects should not be at Paris, as well as in other parts of France…earnestly… represent to them the necessity of the most cautious behaviour during the present disturbances, and that must be particularly careful, both in word and action, to avoid giving any reasonable ground of offence to any of the different parties; into which that kingdom is at present divided.

By 1791, increasing disruption and antagonism to foreigners had already led to a marked fall in tourism.

Yet the Revolution did not follow a predictable pattern. Earlier in 1790, by the first anniversary of the storming of the Bastille (a date celebrated on the site of its ruins), many deputies were opposed to further reform, being instead more concerned with consolidating and institutionalizing the gains already achieved. Leadership at that point seemed to be firmly in the hands of a moderate element keen to work with Louis XVI. The absence of ideological drive at this stage of the Revolution was significant,

and a constitutional monarchy might have continued viable if only
Louis and the conservative aristocracy had been willing to support
it – which proved not to be the case in 1791.

Thus, far from being a homogeneous and unilinear process,
with whatever that might have entailed for Paris, the Revolution
developed in fits and starts. Indeed, its location in Paris was
important here, for radical ideas spread as a consequence of the
Revolution. This owed much not only to the ferment of intellectual
activity in the capital, but also the extent to which there was a clear
social character to many of the factional alignments. The conservative groups were dominated by the privileged, and sociocultural
divisions helped to focus and sustain political perceptions.

The Revolution, which became more radical in 1792, brought
much destruction. Royal sites and monuments were natural targets;
for example, the statues of Louis XIV in the Place Vendôme and
the Place des Victoires. The Place du Trône (now the Place de
la Nation) was in 1794 renamed the Place du Trône-Renversé
('toppled') and became the site of a very busy guillotine, the victims
of which are commemorated in the nearby Picpus Cemetery. The
statue of Henry IV on the Pont Neuf was destroyed in 1792. The
royal corpses from Saint-Denis were exhumed and reburied in
a common grave in 1793, while the urn containing Louis XIV's
heart preserved in the Church of Saint-Paul-Saint-Louis, now
better known as Saint-Paul in the Marais, was melted down and
the heart destroyed. The Sainte-Chapelle at Vincennes was looted
and damaged, with many stained glass windows destroyed. So
also with the Bastille, which by late 1789 had been demolished
and some of its stone used for the Pont de la Concorde. Today, its
grand plan is marked by paving stones in the Place de la Bastille.

The rejection of Christianity by the Revolutionary state meant
that new construction projects for churches such as La Madeleine

were stopped. Monasteries and nunneries were seized and churches repurposed; Notre-Dame became a Temple of Reason, as did the abbey church at Montmartre (the rest of the abbey being destroyed); Saint-Gervais-Saint-Protais became a Temple of Youth. The Benedictine priory dedicated to Saint-Martin-des-Champs became the site of the Conservatoire National des Arts et Métiers. Sainte-Chapelle became a warehouse for storing flour, and Saint-Julien-le-Pauvre for animal feed. The tower of the abbey church at Montmartre was used as a semaphore station. The royal chapel of the Oratoire du Louvre became an arms depot, and the nunnery at Val-de-Grâce a military hospital. The newly completed church dedicated to Saint Geneviève was turned into a Panthéon to 'receive the bodies of great men who died in the period of French liberty'. Today many Parisian streets and place names reflect the past role of the Church, including the sites taken over in the 1790s – as in the Boulevard des Capucines south of the Opéra. Once they had been seized by the state, the extensive grounds of the monasteries with their gardens and orchards were sold to private developers or used for governmental purposes. This was just one aspect of the extensive disruption of the 1790s, which included violent politics, a costly war and an altered service economy as well as the total transformation of education, poor relief and healthcare systems.

Using the Revolutionary Tribunal established in March 1793 and the Committee of Public Safety founded on 6 April, which Maximilien Robespierre joined in July, the Montagnards who had gained power launched a fully fledged Terror in July of that year. This regime denounced all obstacles as the work of nefarious 'enemies of the Revolution'. The Terror was radical, both in its objectives and in the sense of being associated with the *sans-culottes*, but its claim to represent the common people was mostly just another way of keeping order. In fact, the people were not trusted.

Between the creation of the National Convention in September 1792 and its dissolution in the autumn of 1795, no legislative elections took place; only at the local level were a few assemblies convened for municipal and judicial purposes. Apart from the abortive constitution of 1793, the Convention was not prepared to give ordinary people a voice by letting them elect their deputies: elections offered the possibility of democracy, but the new elites thwarted this process with a two-tier procedure intended to filter out popular elements. Moreover, the press was curbed.

The legislation issued by the Revolutionary governments brought no real improvements for the poor, because France lacked the necessary wealth and tax base to support an effective and generous national welfare system. Without economic growth, the secular philosophies of change and improvement were flawed, and it is not surprising that most radical thinkers were sceptical about the appeal of their views to the bulk of the population – indeed, whatever their stated belief in the sovereignty of the people, hostile to what they viewed as popular superstition and conservatism. In 1793, Louis de Saint-Just, a prominent member of the Committee of Public Safety who was later dubbed the Angel of Death, asserted that 'men must be made what they should be'. There was little public appetite for this sort of imposed public virtue, which, besides being impractical, was largely irrelevant to the problems of most people.

On 27 July 1794, the prospect of fresh purges – held out by Robespierre in a speech on 26 July – led to the coup known as Thermidor 9, named after the month in the Revolutionary calendar. Denounced in the National Convention as a tyrant, Robespierre was arrested at once along with his close allies, including Saint-Just. Declared outlaws, they were executed the following evening in the Place de la Révolution, with no rising mounted to save them. In what was known as the Thermidorian

Reaction, a less radical regime took their place, leading in turn, in 1795, to the creation of the Directory government. Ironically, the Thermidorians and the Directory can be seen as another form of extremism, that of an extreme ideological centre. The Jacobin Clubs were closed in 1794–5, while the National Guard, which had been radical since the summer of 1792, became a force of propertied order and helped to defeat uprisings in 1795, notably the insurrection of 12 Germinal (1 April), a rising of the poor in Paris, and that of 1 Prairial (20 May).

Although the Directory had a bicameral legislature and a system of checks and balances, real power rested among its five Directors. However, the political centre, the base of the Directory, was divided, and, in very difficult circumstances, was under challenge from both left and right. This instability was exacerbated by both elections and conspiracies.

In 1795, Napoleon used his troops and far more than the legendary 'whiff of grapeshot' to crush a rising by royalists, of whom about 300 were killed. The bullet holes from his troops can still be seen at the Église Saint-Roch today. The 2002 French miniseries *Napoléon* depicts this battle vividly, offering modern viewers another reminder that the Revolution meant much violence on the streets of Paris.

Alongside political reaction, from 1794 there was a cultural turning towards elitism – reflected in, among other things, fashionable clothing – and the renaming of Paris landmarks began anew. The Place de la Révolution became the Place de la Concorde in 1795. However, this shift did not mean a simple return to pre-Revolutionary circumstances. Instead there was an opening of various sites to the public, including parts of the Louvre in 1793 and, four years later, the library in the Arsenal building (originally established in 1757).

Despite emigration due to the Revolution, Paris remained a major city. In 1800, at about 550,000 people, it was the fifth most populated in the world after Beijing, London (950,000), Guangzhou and Constantinople. Day-to-day life continued alongside the disruptions of revolution and war. Grenoble-born Stendhal, who came to Paris as a young man in 1799 and spent much of the Napoleonic period there, sometimes serving the government, observed in his *Love* (1822): 'A young man of Paris takes in a mistress as a sort of slave, destined above all to satisfy his vanity. If she resists the demands of this dominating passion he leaves her….To find love in Paris you have to go down to the classes where the lack of education and vanity, and the struggle with basic needs, have left more energy to survive.'

France in the late 1790s was a country under enormous strain, divided politically and pressed hard by the war; the Directory was discredited by division and unpopular. The electoral franchise remained very broad and the level of participation was reasonably high; elections in 1798 produced a large group of radical deputies, but the Directory annulled many of the results because the ethos and practice of participatory politics threatened the stability of elite power. This precarious situation encouraged its overthrow in 1799 when Napoleon, who had been busy with an unsuccessful attempt to conquer Egypt, abandoned his army there in order to flee back to France by sea. The problems affecting the Directory represented an opportunity for him to evade responsibility for his failures in the Middle East, bringing to bear his considerable skill as a propagandist as he rapidly seized power.

The Directory swiftly succumbed to a coup mounted by Napoleon and others on 9 November (18 Brumaire, according to the Revolutionary calendar), and he became First Consul and

General-in-Chief. From a certain perspective this might seem like a very neat outcome, the seamless and necessary product of strategy and circumstance – however, that was far from being the case. There had been bungling on the part of both conspirators and opponents, and a loss of nerve by Napoleon. It was far from inevitable that the Directory would fall rather than rally and overcome the challenge, as it had done in 1797.

So also with the aftermath. The divisions that had been deepened by the Terror, as well as the continuation of the war, had made it virtually impossible to establish any sort of stable liberal regime after 1795. Consequently, an outcome similar to that of 1799 had always been likely – although it might perhaps have been a stronger form of civilian rule, rather than that of Napoleon. The bourgeois turned to Napoleon because he represented the safeguarding of, if not political freedom, at least the status and power that were challenged by elections and electioneering.

The regime Napoleon inaugurated in 1799 lasted until 1814, with a brief revival in 1815. Paris saw many changes under his rule. Alongside new buildings and infrastructure – including the opening in 1804 of the cemetery of Père-Lachaise, a sanitary alternative to the old city centre graveyards – Napoleon brought destruction. The demolition or repurposing of church buildings continued: the sixteenth-century Church of Saint-Jacques-de-la-Boucherie was pulled down in 1802 apart from its tower, which was used as a weather station. The Temple, which had been a prison since the disbandment of the Knights Templar in 1312, was demolished in 1808. Napoleon decided in 1806 that the church of La Madeleine would be completed as a temple to the glory of the Grand Army. However, he returned the Panthéon to the Church and commissioned from Antoine-Jean Gros the *Glorification of Sainte Geneviève* that decorates the inside of its cupola.

Napoleon's relationship with the capital was mixed. He made it a centre of imperial display – notably, his coronation as emperor in Notre-Dame in 1804 – but it was also a source of potential opposition, both republican and royalist. There was an assassination attempt in the Rue Nicaise on Christmas Eve 1800 by a royalist bomber, and an unsuccessful Republican coup in 1812. The Café des Deux-Anges on the Rue du Bac became a meeting place for royalist conspirators.

Napoleon's real court was his army, and he spent much time away on campaign. In Paris he remained mostly in the Tuileries, his official residence, where in 1806 he constructed a triumphal arch, the Arc de Triomphe du Carrousel, as well as a new wing that faced onto a new street: the Rue de Rivoli, named for one of his victories. Built in 1806–7 and still standing today, the Châtelet commemorated Napoleon's triumphs.

The first stone of the Arc de Triomphe was laid in 1806, but it was still incomplete in 1810 when Napoleon's second wife, Marie-Louise of Austria, made her triumphal entry. A mock-up had to be erected, made of painted canvas supported by scaffolding. The marble arch was originally supposed to be topped with the Horses of Saint Mark, which Napoleon had seized from Venice, but France had to return them after his defeat, and instead it is topped by copies.

More generally, Napoleon, seeking to make Paris a new Rome, embellished the city with various paintings and sculptures looted during his conquests, all the way back to the start of his campaigning in Italy. To the victor the spoils: he sought to make the Louvre a universal museum, the Napoleon Museum, unmatched anywhere in the world. Under pressure from foreign powers in the aftermath of his defeat, many of these works had to be returned, but some remain including, in the Louvre, Paolo Veronese's *Wedding at Cana*.

Napoleon's campaigns are commemorated in the Musée de l'Armée at the Invalides, where his tomb is also located.

Like many dictators – particularly wartime dictators – Napoleon conceived numerous schemes that were never completed or, as with the Arc de Triomphe, not until later. Others were not even started, such as his plan to erect a large palace for his son on the site of a convent that had been destroyed in the Revolution.

Napoleon also recast the administration of the city, changing the *quartiers* of the *ancien régime* into arrondissements run by mayors who, like the two prefects, were appointed rather than elected. The affordability of bread was supported while hospitals, watchmen and sewerage were all improved; care was taken in the development of new cemeteries, notably in the Catacombs created from stone quarries. Three bridges – those of Iéna, Austerlitz and the Arts – were constructed and industrial plant was encouraged. Meanwhile, tourism from Britain briefly resumed following the Peace of Amiens in 1802, but was cut short in 1803 when war resumed and British visitors were interned by Napoleon.

The city remained the capital of a global empire. During 1814–15 Napoleon's defeat, followed by return and then a further defeat, led to three changes of government being imposed by force. In the course of these, Paris avoided the threatened devastation: there was nothing to match the British burning of public buildings that took place in Washington in 1814, let alone the destruction in Moscow during the French invasion of 1812. In 1814, having defeated a French force at Fère-Champenoise on 25 March, the Austrians and Prussians marched on Paris, ignoring Napoleon's position on their flank. The attackers' 107,000 men faced only about 23,000 defenders, who were driven back into the Paris suburbs on 30 March. Negotiations opened the following day, and Napoleon abdicated on 6 April.

A reputation for cuisine

FRENCH FOOD WAS IMPRINTED ON THE EUROPEAN CONSCIOUSNESS as a result of occupations from 1814 to 1818. Brillat-Savarin, a renowned gourmet of the eighteenth century, recalled:

> When the Britons, Germans, Teutons, Cimmerians, and Scythians made their irruption into France, they brought with them a rare voracity and stomachs of no common capacity....Soon the Queen City became nothing but an enormous refectory. Those invaders ate in restaurants, eating-houses, inns, taverns, at open-air stalls, and even in the streets. They gorged themselves with meat, fish, game, truffles, pastry, and especially with our fruit. They drank with an avidity equal to their appetite, and always ordered the dearest wines. —*A Handbook of Gastronomy: Brillat-Savarin's Physiologie du goût*, 1884

He was subsequently welcomed back at the Tuileries on the evening of 20 March 1815, without a shot having been fired. The unpopularity of Louis XVIII, who had fled Paris the previous night, was an important factor in this, as were Napoleon's rapid advance and the uncertain response of the French military. After experiencing total defeat at Waterloo on 18 June, Napoleon reached Paris on the 21st but was thwarted by developing opposition there and left the Élysée Palace on the 25th, taking refuge at Malmaison. He would eventually return to Paris to be buried – and then only because a king, Louis Philippe, decided it was appropriate.

In 1815, noting the devastation caused by the advancing Prussians, Major William Turner predicted: 'That infernal city

Paris will be attacked and no doubt pillaged for it is a debt we owe to the whole of Europe.' The Right Bank and the northern approach were strongly defended around Montmartre, and Marshal Blücher decided to advance on the less well-protected Left Bank. On 2 July, he established himself on the heights of Meudon and at the village of Issy. A French dawn attack on Issy was repulsed on 3 July, while the advancing British forces were building a bridge across the Seine at Argenteuil.

That day, the French agreed to evacuate Paris. Anglo-Prussian forces occupied the city without resistance on 7 July and Louis XVIII returned on the 8th, being greeted with singularly little popular enthusiasm. From his base in Paris, Wellington took charge of the occupation, which lasted until reparations were paid in 1818. He thwarted Blücher's plan to demolish the Pont d'Iéna, built in 1806–13 to commemorate the victory of 1806 over Prussia. The capital, however, now commemorated the Allied triumph; on 10 July, Tsar Alexander I, Francis I of Austria and Frederick William III of Prussia reached Paris on a journey of victory.

Paris would look very different today if not for the fact that in 1814 and 1815, it did not serve as a fortified city – instead, in 1815, defeat at Waterloo led to its speedy fall, sparing the city the devastation that would certainly have come from the use of cannon and looting by troops. There was no precursor to the Prussian bombardment of 1871. Cannon in 1814 and 1815 were, of course, less powerful than later on, but the damage done by the short British bombardment of Copenhagen in 1807 demonstrated the effects they could have. Paris had been spared the worst, as it would largely be again during the two world wars a century later.

Chapter 9

Restored Monarchy to War, 1815–1870

Along the Canal Saint-Martin in north-eastern Paris, it is possible to take a walk in the early nineteenth century. Authorized by Napoleon in 1802 in order to provide Paris with fresh water from the river Ourcq, building continued on the canal until 1825, funded in part by a tax on wine. It had two ports in the city: the Bassin de la Villette, terminating the 108-kilometre (67-mile) Canal de l'Ourcq, opened in 1822, and the Port de l'Arsenal. This was once a busy industrial thoroughfare, until its job of transporting goods was taken over by the railways.

Among the many buildings, roads and quarters in Paris dating to this period, the railway stations were perhaps the most striking and significant to contemporary residents. They represented change in the broader sense as well as major alterations in the layout of the city, with roads converging on them and much else swept aside for their benefit.

A passenger railway line, funded by bankers, opened between Paris and Saint-Germain in 1837. In 1842, a government plan saw the state agree to contribute heavily to the construction of several trunk lines. Their convergence on Paris, however, created major problems for links between the regions, with longer journeys often having to be made via the capital.

Today, two very different Paris station buildings command the attention of tourists: the Gare du Nord, which is still in use and currently the busiest station in Europe, and the Musée d'Orsay, formerly the Gare d'Orsay. The latter was only a minor station – the terminus of the Orléans line – and narrowly escaped demolition in the 1970s before being transformed into one of Europe's largest museums, reopening in 1986.

The Gare du Nord is not a typical French railway station, in that its role as a hub for the Eurostar services affects access (as well as encouraging pickpocketing), and it is presently in a somewhat seedy state. France's second-busiest station, the Gare de Lyon, is more elegant. Begun in 1847 and opened in 1849, it was, like most stations, a product of compromise: the company originally hoped the line could run to the more central Place de la Bastille, but the intervening Rue de Lyon blocked access. Rebuilt in 1855, the station served as a cannon foundry in 1870 during the Franco-Prussian War. Now, having been rebuilt and expanded anew in 1900, it invites you to escape from Paris to the south.

There was an attempt to turn back the clock to pre-Revolutionary days under the regime known as the Restoration, which began in 1814 and gathered pace after Napoleon's final defeat the following year. The Restoration took its name from the return of Bourbon rule, first with Louis XVIII (r. 1814–24) and then with his brother Charles X (r. 1824–30). Many statues that had been destroyed by the Revolutionaries were replaced; the cell in the Conciergerie where Marie Antoinette had been held before her execution was converted into an expiatory chapel; and the existing chapel, which had also been used as a prison cell, was reconsecrated. In 1816, a tomb and chapel within the Sainte-Chapelle at Vincennes were added to hold the remains of Louis, Duke of Enghien, a member of the House of Bourbon who had been shot at Vincennes on the orders of Napoleon in 1804. Royalist sympathy led to the installation of sculptures of Louis XVI and Marie Antoinette kneeling in prayer in the basilica at Saint-Denis, while, although the idea was not pursued, Louis XVIII wanted the Madeleine completed as an expiatory chapel for the sins of the Revolution. The building of the Arc de Triomphe was temporarily abandoned.

The government was generally suspicious of Paris, perceiving it as a centre of Revolutionary sentiment and opposition to staunch Catholicism, but there could be no attempt to move to a new capital (unlike in 1940, when the capital would relocate to Vichy during the German occupation). The occupation by the victorious Allies under the command of the Duke of Wellington was initially intended to last for five years, but came to an end in 1818 with the payment of substantial reparations.

Louis XVIII resided mostly in the Tuileries Palace; Versailles was not used. Paris, however, remained a source of menace owing to incidents like the assassination in 1820 of Louis's nephew Charles, Duke of Berry, who was killed while leaving the Opéra by a Bonapartist veteran called Louis Pierre Louvel.

Louis's successor, his reactionary and difficult brother Charles X, was unpopular in Paris – all the more so from 1827, when disruptive heckling during his review of the National Guard there prompted him to disband it – and the liberal opposition dominated the city returns in that year's election. Parisian representatives played an important role in the subsequent opposition to the government in the Chamber of Deputies, and the Revolution that overthrew Charles in 1830 began with crowd action in the gardens of the Palais-Royal.

The failure of the regular troops to thwart an armed rising in Paris that July can be attributed in part to the regulars' deficiencies

20 ARROND^TS

PLAN DE PARI

LUSTRÊ 1864

80 QUARTIERS

in street fighting, although a shortage of food and ammunition were contributing factors. This failure has to be set in the wider context of a widely disliked and poorly directed government that had attempted to reverse the verdicts of recent elections. Much of the army was dissatisfied with Charles's policies and many of the more loyal units were away during the summer of 1830, taking part in the conquest of Algeria – consequently there were only 12,000 troops on hand near Paris, not all of whom could be relied upon. Large numbers of them deserted, while Charles failed to provide clear leadership and Marshal Marmont was simply not up to the task.

Despite the rebels' lack of training, equipment and discipline – and the fact that about 600 of them were killed compared to only

---

Tourism renewed

AFTER NAPOLEON ABDICATED IN 1814 THERE WAS ANOTHER short-lived burst in tourism, but it was not until after Waterloo that a sustained revival occurred. France, however, had changed. British tourists who visited it after the Restoration were conscious that they were seeing a different world to that toured by their pre-Revolutionary predecessors, and that the intervening changes could not be reversed. More critically, Honoré de Balzac in the 1839 portion of his novel *Lost Illusions* (trans. Herbert J. Hunt, Penguin, 1971) referred to 'those squalid rooms which are the disgrace of Paris where despite all its pretensions to elegance there is not yet a single hotel in which any wealthy traveller can feel at home'. Balzac's home can be visited in the Passy quarter, where he rented under his housekeeper's name in order to evade his creditors.

---

about 150 soldiers – they managed to seize and hold the initiative. Charles left the palace of Saint-Cloud and, having been told that Versailles was not safe, fled to Rambouillet. There he abdicated in favour of his grandson, only to have that disposition ignored. He subsequently departed for the United Kingdom by packet steamer and was replaced by Louis Philippe (r. 1830–48) of the Orléanist branch of the Bourbon dynasty.

Two years later, the new government was more successful in suppressing a greatly outnumbered republican insurrection. This had arisen in response to rumours that the government was poisoning the wells, causing an epidemic of cholera. Barricades were established by 3,000 or so insurgents, most of whom were working class; the action was concentrated in eastern Paris and the more central Faubourg Saint-Martin. A witness, Victor Hugo, used these events as the basis for his novel *Les Misérables* (1862). In 1834 further republican riots were suppressed with great brutality, albeit against less serious resistance. Between these outbreaks of violence, which included an assassination attempt on the king in 1835, there was a continual sense of possible insurrection that coloured the image of Paris in France and abroad, undermining the authorities' attempts to present cohesion.

Under the 'July Monarchy' of Louis Philippe, who, like his predecessor, resided in the Tuileries, Paris was not a centre of court splendour; but his modest style, in contrast with the grandeur of Charles X, appeared appropriate. There were some enhancements to the cityscape, notably the unveiling of a 220-ton obelisk in the middle of the Place de la Concorde in 1836. This object had been a gift to Louis Philippe from Muhammad Ali of Egypt, and it seemed obvious to the king that it should be displayed in the city rather than in the gardens of Versailles. The obelisk accomplished an unproblematic remastering of a space that had been uneasily associated with the guillotine, and it linked Paris to a civilization even more ancient than Rome.

During the Restoration there had been limited improvement of public works in the city, but this became more of a priority from 1833 – in part owing to the availability of government grants but also thanks to the drive of Claude-Philibert, Count Rambuteau, Prefect of the Département of the Seine from 1833 to 1848. It was Rambuteau who set in motion the process of urban regeneration that is popularly associated with Baron Haussmann (discussed below); streets were widened in order to allow for better circulation of air and, it was hoped, lower the risk of disease. One such street was later renamed in honour of Rambuteau, who also improved the sewerage, water supply and gas lighting and arranged for the installation of more than 400 public urinals.

The Arc de Triomphe was completed in 1836 and the carriage bringing Napoleon's body to the Invalides on his return from Saint Helena passed underneath it. The Colonne de Juillet in the Place de la Bastille commemorates the Parisians killed in the 1830 uprising, with many of their names on the column and their bodies in the crypt below. The Rue de Rivoli, begun under Napoleon I, was at last finished in 1848; Napoleon III would later extend it into the Marais. A different type of commemoration can be seen above the peristyle of the Panthéon, which Louis Philippe converted from church to necropolis: sculptures by David d'Angers show Liberty presenting laurel crowns to the Nation with which to acclaim her great men. This is somewhat different to Eugène Delacroix's dramatic painting *Liberty Leading the People* (1830), held in the Louvre, which depicts Liberty as a determined female warrior.

This was also a period of resumed church-building, which produced a number of impressive churches in a variety of styles.

The machine infernale

IN 1835, LOUIS PHILIPPE WAS ATTACKED ON THE BOULEVARD
du Temple while on the way to his annual review of the
Paris National Guard. Giuseppe Mario Fieschi, a republican
Revolutionary and veteran, had made a volley gun of twenty-
five gun barrels that could be fired simultaneously. The king
was only lightly wounded, but eighteen other people were
killed. Fieschi himself was injured by some of the barrels
malfunctioning, and was soon captured and guillotined.

They include the neo-Gothic Sainte-Clotilde, built in 1846–56
and a good example of the stained glass of its era. There was also
restoration of some older churches, as at Saint-Germain-des-Prés.

Meanwhile, markets and public spaces were remodelled and
improved and sanitation addressed, necessarily so in light of cholera
and other diseases. Between 1814 and 1832, 15,000 metres of sewers
were constructed; an impressive 62,682 more were added from 1832
to 1840, and then a further 27,321 from 1841 to 1847. Although
this represented significant progress, conditions were often bleak
for the workers whose labour expanded Paris. Masons typically
travelled long distances, often from the Limousin, in order to work
in the capital for the year until winter closed in.

Throughout all of this, Parisians lived with the constant threat
of violent attack. In the 1830s and early 1840s the city was extensively refortified with a ring of detached forts to provide defence in
depth, partly by increasing the line of investment that the besiegers
had to man while, at the same time, providing cover and strength
for a field force – thus serving as a large entrenched camp. The
36-kilometre-long (22 miles) city walls built between 1841 and 1845,

which included a moat, would not be demolished until after the First World War. As with so much in the history of Paris, there was a complex network of political and financial considerations at play in these developments. The fortification programme stalled from 1833 for budget reasons but resumed in 1841, and was finished in 1844 at a cost of 145 million francs. This was in large part thanks to France having climbed down from an international crisis in 1840, one that had revealed the country's vulnerability.

An uprising by Parisian workers in February 1848 forced out Louis Philippe and his Orléanist monarchy, not least because the elderly king was reluctant to use regular troops to suppress it. He abdicated in favour of his grandson, Philip, Count of Paris, but although there was support for this idea in the National Assembly, public opinion in Paris was opposed and the republicans seized power. The Second Republic was proclaimed from the Hôtel de Ville, as the Third Republic would be in 1870. In July 1848 the throne of Louis Philippe was ceremoniously burnt in the Place du Trône (which would later, in 1880, be renamed the Place de la Nation). Today, Philip's descendants continue to claim their right to the throne – the current claimant is Jean Carl Pierre Marie d'Orléans, who (to very few) is Jean IV but styles himself the Count of Paris.

During that summer of 1848, when Parisian workers took to the barricades against the abolition of the national workshops (a recently established form of publicly funded work), they were crushed by the Second Republic's minister of war, a Parisian called General Louis-Eugène Cavaignac. There was, alongside ideology and politics, a clear geographical-social edge to this conflict. Cavaignac used peasant regular troops and 100,000 National Guardsmen (who had refused to defend the king in February) to fight his way through the city's barricades against the insurgents' so-called Army of Despair. Approximately 1,600 troops and 10,000 insurgents were killed. This division among the working classes was more apparent than Karl Marx's claim that the fighting in Paris was 'the first great battle...between the two classes that split modern society'. With Cavaignac's troops fighting their way to the Place de la Bastille, the centre of the rebellion, radicalism was crushed. Cavaignac became Chief of the Executive Power, running the government, which in part involved banning radical newspapers, until the elections that December. The victor was Napoleon's nephew, Louis-Napoleon, who, with 74 per cent of the vote, was elected president of the Second Republic. An attempted insurrection in Paris by the radical Montagnards was crushed in June 1849 and Napoleon consolidated his position with a coup in December 1851, dissolving the National Assembly and becoming Napoleon III in 1852. Resistance to his coup in Paris was rapidly overcome, with about 200 citizens killed by troops. An authoritarian constitution with Napoleon as president came into force in January 1852, and that December he became the Emperor Napoleon III.

At this point Paris, like London, was a European city with over one million residents, and for both places that created major problems of management. It was not simply a matter of numbers. Living standards were a serious issue both for those directly affected by poverty or homelessness and, more broadly, for a city threatened by disease. Between a quarter and a fifth of workers lived in crowded multi-storey houses affected by damp, with pinched rooms, low ceilings and frequently no fireplace or wallpaper. Nevertheless, despite a cholera epidemic in 1832 that killed 19,000 people, the population of Paris grew sharply under the July Monarchy, rising from 861,436 in 1831 to 1,226,980 in 1846. While providing cheap labour, this growth exacerbated social problems in the city. In 1848, with a reference to the filth in the city, the journalist Henri Lecouturier captured a need for reform: 'Most of the streets of this wonderful Paris are…filthy and permanently wet with pestilential water.' Eleven years later, a parliamentary report claimed that 'air, light and healthiness' had recently been brought to Paris – yet this was far from complete.

The achievements of Georges-Eugène Haussmann (Baron Haussmann), prefect of the Seine and director of public works from 1853 to 1870, have generally been characterized as a response to deficiencies in the security of Paris. These were important, and straight boulevards did provide a clearer field of fire, but public order and security were not seen only in terms of rioting crowds. Microbes were also threats. Haussmann addressed the city's water and gas supply, lighting systems and transport flow, while a municipal morgue was built on the Île de la Cité at what is now the Square de l'Île-de-France. Today, part of the massive extension to the sewers under Haussmann can be visited in an area of Les Égouts accessible at the Quai d'Orsay, where there is a Museum of Sewers.

Bridges were rebuilt during the programme of modernization, and trees added. The widening of streets continued, as begun by Rambuteau, as well as the building of new boulevards and bridges and the laying out of parks including the Parc Montsouris, the Parc des Buttes-Chaumont, the Bois de Boulogne, the Bois de Vincennes and about twenty smaller parks. The Arc de Triomphe gained seven new radiating avenues to add to the existing five. Major buildings were enhanced by a replanning that involved significant demolition, as with the expansion of the square near the Hôtel de Ville – a step accompanied, significantly, by the building of two barracks nearby. Troops were to be available to preserve order within the city. Much of the crowded Île de la Cité was cleared to make way for an administrative complex incorporating the Hôtel-Dieu (hospital), far larger law courts and a barracks, now a police prefecture.

Among the casualties of demolition was the house in which Haussmann himself had been born, as well as an entire working-class district that was cleared to make way for the Boulevard de Sébastopol (its name commemorating a success in the Crimean War). Many of the eighteenth-century displays in the Musée Carnavalet were sourced from the destruction of better properties. The sweeping powers granted to Haussmann and the funds provided to make all of this work possible were a reflection of Napoleon III's desire for an exemplary and glorious modernization that would bring prestige – although the monarch also wasted plenty of money on conspicuous consumption, as is apparent in his apartments, which can be visited in the Louvre.

Redevelopment in the 1840s had been limited, even thwarted by an absence of legal mechanisms, but now it was made easier for the city to purchase land. The preservation of city centre slums was not part of Napoleon's vision for the city, but opposition to street-widening in more exalted quarters was difficult to overcome. Here financial benefit played a role, with rising land prices offering tempting opportunities for private investment in a construction boom that stimulated the city's economy as a whole. A majestic city was to be reflected in an effective geometry of movement through new boulevards amid the accompanying display of squares and monuments, with the limestone for the new housing brought to the capital by rail. New boulevards included Magenta, Malesherbes, Raspail, Saint-Michel, and what is now Voltaire; Solferino gave its name to a street where the Socialist Party long had its headquarters; and new squares included today's Place de la République and Place Simone Veil.

Like Napoleon I, Napoleon III commemorated 'his' military victories in place names. Although he had not in fact been present at the Alma (1854), a Crimean War battle after which a bridge and nearby square were named, he was in overall command at Solferino (1859) and Magenta (1859), both of which were fought in Italy. The Pont de l'Alma was replaced in 1970 but an original statue of one of the soldiers has been preserved beneath the new bridge.

The first of the city's large department stores developed around this time. Le Bon Marché was founded in 1838 and transformed from 1852 by Aristide Boucicaut, who oversaw the move to its current site in 1869. The annual income of the store rose from 500,000 francs in 1852 to 72 million by 1877. La Samaritaine followed in 1869, and the Galeries Lafayette in 1894. Meanwhile, Baron Haussmann had been dismissed as prefect of the Seine in January 1870; the cost of his projects as well as the dirigiste nature of his planning decisions had drawn strong criticism in some quarters, including from Émile Ollivier, who became prime minister after the 1869 elections.

Paris rapidly grew through migration from other parts of France. An 1859 extension of the city limits incorporated all or parts of twenty-four suburban communes, raising the number of arrondissements from twelve to twenty. As a result, the city's area more than doubled and by 1870 its population quadrupled to almost two million, many of whom were living in terrible poverty. The expansion boosted revenue, as did an increase in city taxes. The loss in 1860 of the Wall of the *Ferme générale*, built in 1784–91, was met with indifference as it had been a toll boundary rather than a defensive structure.

After the annexation, some urban areas that had fallen out of favour, such as Notre-Dame-des-Champs (near the Luxembourg Gardens), were gentrified and new ones became popular with the middle classes. One of these was the Parc Monceau, where in 1871 many Communards were massacred. The Buttes-Chaumont was landscaped into a park, the first on the northern edge of the city.

Some areas of the new arrondissements, such as Vaugirard, were already populous. Others retained rural and village features for a while, including Auteuil, which remains relatively low-density, and, very differently, Belleville, also formerly an area of vineyards. The Bois de Boulogne, a royal forest, was given to the city by Napoleon in 1852 and Haussmann oversaw its transformation. Its surrounding wall was demolished and new features, including the Avenue de l'Impératrice (from 1929, Rue Foch) and the Longchamp racecourse, were built under his supervision.

Louis Wuhrer's 1871 map captured the expansion, emphasizing the extension of Paris and the new roads. In contrast, F. Dufour's *Nouveau Paris Monumental. Itineraire Pratique de l'Étranger dans Paris* (1878), which is shown on pages 150–1, focused mainly on the traditional in the shape of prominent buildings, although it did show the railway links intended to bring visitors.

The arrival of the railways had a tremendous impact on Paris, transforming both the actual infrastructure of the city and its relationship to the rest of France and abroad. Railway stations – of which the last major one, the Gare de Lyon, was in full operation by 1857 – took up a lot of space and tended to have dramatic façades that dominated everything around them, like that of Jakob Hittorff's Gare du Nord (completed in 1846). Railway yards and viaducts were also large, physically imposing structures. The Vincennes railway line, opened in 1859, linked the Gare de Vincennes at the Place de la Bastille (demolished in 1984) to Verneuil-l'Étang via Vincennes. The arcades of the 1.5-kilometre-long (1 mile) Viaduc de Bastille, with its sixty-four vaults, overlooked the Avenue Daumesnil. Other stations followed, notably the Beaux-Arts-style Gare d'Orsay, built in 1898–1900. The Paris Métro was originally intended in part to be a filling in of the rail system.

Other forms of transport posed different issues – for example, the horse-drawn bus, which appeared after the establishment of the Compagnie Générale des Omnibus in 1855 and produced much muck. The bus was followed by the horse-drawn tram, which ran on rails. By 1878 Paris had at least 78,000 horses, and as late as 1912 there were still about 56,000, with the Bon Marché department store alone maintaining more than 150 horses at its underground stables to transport customers and goods. The police, fire service and post office all had horses, as did the army units. Plentiful and inexpensive horsemeat was a major byproduct. When the Métro opened in 1900 it helped to ensure the end of horse buses, but horses themselves remained important to the city's economy until mid-century.

Facilities for tourists had improved greatly. New railway station hotels provided meals and rooms, but more central accommodation was also becoming available. When the Grand Hôtel du Louvre opened in 1855 (see plate XIV), its 700 rooms took standards to a new level, and it was rapidly emulated. The same entrepreneurs, Isaac and Émile Pereire, and designer, Alfred Armand, were responsible for the 800-room Le Grand Hôtel, opened in 1862 (it had a separate floor for servants). Older hotels had been much smaller. Founded in 1815, principally for British tourists, the Hôtel Meurice relocated to a setting on the Rue de Rivoli in 1835. As of 1891 it could only house 200 guests, but it would be enlarged in the 1900s. The new emphasis on scale and standardization were part of what Edmond de Goncourt in 1870 dubbed the 'Americanization' of Paris. It was seen within France as the basis for a new version of the Parisian-driven modernization that was generally unwelcome at all levels of provincial society.

Dickens in Paris

'I SEE A BEAUTIFUL CITY AND A BRILLIANT PEOPLE RISING FROM THIS
abyss, and, in their struggles to be truly free, in their triumphs
and defeats, I see the evil of this time and of the previous time
of which this is the natural birth, gradually making expiation
for itself and wearing out.' In *A Tale of Two Cities* (1859), Charles
Dickens gave Sydney Carton an exemplary final speech as he
faced the decapitating Terror of the French Revolution. Familiar
with Paris and its culture, Dickens also presented an attractive
view of the city's dynamism in *Bleak House* (1852–3).

Among other cultural developments, Paris provided the
setting for the development of the murder mystery with Edgar
Allan Poe's 'The Murders in the Rue Morgue' (1841), a locked-
room puzzle set in a fictional street. Poe, an American, had
never actually visited Paris. Victor Hugo's *The Hunchback of
Notre-Dame* (1831) was a different sort of mystery: one suggesting
dark, hidden truths, but set in the fifteenth century. That theme
of shadowy secrecy recurs in much of the popular literature surrounding Paris even today – Lucy Foley's *The Paris Apartment*
(2020) is a recent example. The timeless contrast between the
external (buildings) and the internal (people) is frequently to
the fore, perhaps even more so than in novels set in London or
New York.

Zola ended his 1880 novel *Nana*, which is set during the late
1860s, with a mob repeatedly shouting 'To Berlin! To Berlin! To
Berlin!' – a depiction of the mounting chaos that would ultimately,
by way of the Franco-Prussian War, lead to the collapse of the
Second Empire: '[T]he crowds…surging along like flocks of sheep

being driven to the slaughter-house at night. These shadowy masses rolling by in a dizzying human flood exhaled a sense of terror, a pitiful premonition of future massacres…"What utter folly this war is! What bloodthirsty stupidity!"…A great breath of despair came up from the boulevard and filled out the curtains.'

Chapter 10

Belle Époque,
1871–1914

Following heavy defeat by Germany in 1870 and his own capitulation at Sedan, Napoleon III's rule was replaced by the Third Republic after crowds of Parisians occupied the Chamber of Deputies. On 4 September, the new republic was proclaimed from the Hôtel de Ville.

The change ensured that the war would continue. The new Government of National Defence, determined not to surrender territory to Germany, discovered a role through continued resistance. Léon Gambetta, the new Minister of the Interior who had proclaimed the Republic, mobilized the Paris *Garde Nationale*.

Unwilling to concede generous terms, the Germans advanced on Paris, which they had surrounded by 19 September. There was no attempt, however, to storm the city, a difficult target. Moltke, the German commander, intended to rely instead on starvation, but Bismarck, the German chancellor, persuaded Wilhelm I to add bombardment, which began on 5 January 1871. Ten days later, the politician Henry Labouchère noted: 'the cannon make one continuous noise…shells burst in restaurants and maim the waiters…the trenches are in tea-gardens'. The devastating consequences to one of Europe's leading cities suggested to influential contemporaries that conflict had become barbarous and needed to be contained by new laws of war. The new French government, based in Tours, raised forces in what it called a 'national war' to relieve Paris – only to be repeatedly defeated, leading to a transfer of the seat of government to Bordeaux. Meanwhile, attempts to break out of Paris failed: the confidence of republican enthusiasts in a *sortie en masse* proved misplaced. With Paris buffeted by the bombardment and running out of food while war-weariness grew throughout France, an armistice was signed on 28 January; German terms were accepted by the National Assembly in March. This time, unlike in 1815 and 1940, there would be no occupation of the capital.

At around the same time, an insurrection took place in Paris that led to the creation of a revolutionary commune. A mostly working-class radical movement, the Commune issued decrees calling for a range of actions, from the separation of church and state to the abolition of night work in bakeries. Once the war with Germany had ended, however, the government bloodily suppressed the Commune in what became one of the most dramatic episodes in Paris's history. Fighting began over the control of cannon and quickly became bitter, with each side murdering prisoners. Jules Favre, a government supporter, wrote:

> Our soldiers were advancing only slowly, hindered at every step by barricades which they had to outflank by making their way through the houses. The barricade in the Place de la Concorde was formidably high, protected by a deep trench, bristling with guns. General Douay captured it, in spite of the desperate efforts of its defenders.

Jules Pau, another French observer, noted: 'One of the most impressive barricades, as far as the defence was concerned, was the

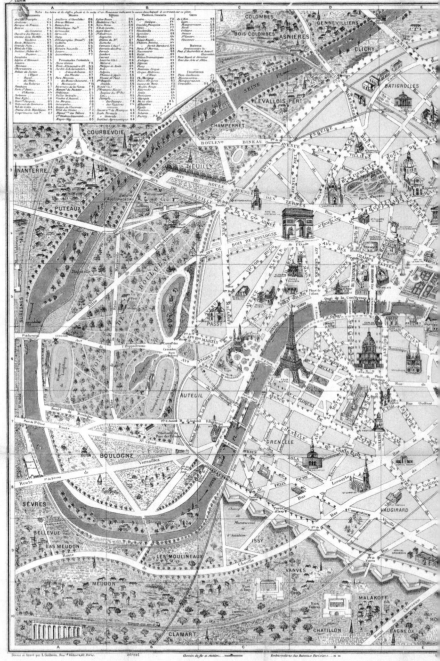

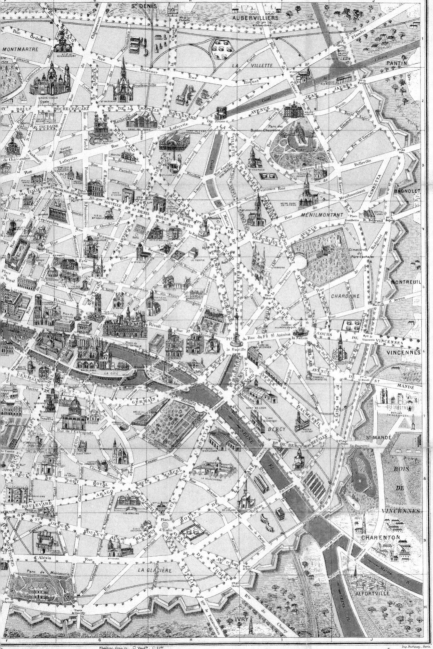

one in the Rue Royale. Equipped with cannon and *mitrailleuses* [machine guns].'

After extensive street fighting from March to May, during which about 10,000 Parisians were killed, about the same number of captives – possibly many more – were shot, some of them at the Mur des Fédérés (Communards' Wall) in the cemetery of Père-Lachaise, a wall that can still be seen. Many of the bodies were left out for a while. Some of the surviving Communards were condemned to forced labour and deported to the South Pacific penal colony of New Caledonia; there was no complete amnesty until 1880.

Earlier, the Communards too had killed their hostages, but in far, far smaller numbers. In Belleville, at the Mur des Otages, is part of a wall where they shot fifty-two priests, nuns and guards; the site is further commemorated in the nearby church of Notre-Dame-des-Otages, constructed in 1936. Georges Darboy, the archbishop, was killed. Many sites of conventional authority were set on fire in the course of the conflict, including the Tuileries, the Palais-Royal and the Hôtel de Ville. Some were rebuilt, but not all, and lasting damage was caused by the failure to replace significant sites such as the Tuileries. The Palais d'Orsay, dating to 1810, had held government offices before being burned down in 1871 – its ruins would later become the site of the Gare d'Orsay.

The bloody outcome of the Commune represented yet another difficult and divisive new chapter in the collective memory of Paris, which subsequent governments would struggle to efface. Karl Marx was clear in his view:

> …working men's Paris, with its Commune, will be for ever celebrated as the glorious harbinger of a new society. Its exter-minators' history has already nailed to that eternal pillory

from which all the prayers of their priests will not avail to redeem them.

The much less sympathetic Zola, who was present in Paris at the time, concentrated on the scale of destruction, which was greater than that seen during the Revolution – indeed, greater than at any time in the city's history, before or since. Even the Viking siege of 885–6 had not devastated the centre. Zola's bestselling novel *The Debacle* (1892) describes the buildings burned by the Communards and their execution by firing squad; the sky glows 'with a murderous, bloody light….It was destruction for destruction's sake so as to bury the ancient, rotten human society beneath the ashes of the world in the hope that a new society would spring up, happy and innocent, in the earthly paradise of primitive legends!….What a hellish city it was…a rolling sea of fiery roofs…the sea of flames.'

Because of concerns about its potential as an instrument of revolution, the National Guard was dissolved in 1872 (it would be reconstituted in 2016 in response to terrorism) and replaced by the regular army. Paris remained under martial law until 1876. And yet a very different impression of 1876 – which was also the year of a republican majority in the elections – can be found in the Musée d'Orsay in the form of Renoir's *Dancing at the Moulin de la Galette* (see plate XIII), which depicts a scene of open-air ease and pleasure. It calls to mind again *The Debacle*, in which Zola juxtaposes the Communards being shot with life 'stirring' for other Parisians as they go for walks and sit outside cafés.

Once order was restored, there was a renewed effort to tame the city. The 1875 Constitution not only left the way open for a monarchy but also acted as a restraint to the representation of Paris in the National Assembly, which remained in Versailles until 1879.

Control of the city was maintained by an appointed prefect rather than an elected mayor. Baron Haussmann's plans were picked up again, and the return to relative peace was celebrated with the holding in 1878 of a World's Fair on the Champ de Mars, which attracted 13 million visitors. The Eiffel Tower was to follow there in 1889 for the Universal Exhibition, which was visited by 32 million people. At 320 metres tall (1,051 feet), it was the world's tallest building until the completion of the Empire State Building in New York in 1931. Eiffel, who had won a design competition to build the tower, made its 18,038 metallic parts at his factory at Levallois-Perret on the outskirts of Paris; they were then moved to the construction site, where they were put together using 2.5 million rivets (see plate XI).

The Sacré-Coeur Basilica, begun in 1875, was built on the highest point of the city as a way of proclaiming the presence of religion in and over Paris. It was not finished until 1914, and not consecrated until 1919. Given the astronomical cost of its neo-Romano-Byzantine styling, which included pointed cupolas and interior mosaics, it is instructive that its best features are the views from the external gallery of the dome and from the terrace in front of the church.

In Montmartre, there is more architectural interest in the church of Saint-Jean-de-Montmartre: designed by Anatole de Baudot and Paul Cottancin, this radical project used reinforced concrete to provide relatively inexpensive strength, as well as to permit thinner walls supporting vaulted ceilings. Built over the course of a decade from 1894 to 1904, it was the first religious building to be made from concrete, and there was much opposition to the construction method – the unfinished church was even threatened with demolition. Ecclesiastical investment in the rapidly growing area of Montmartre also included the restoration of the Church of Saint-Pierre de Montmartre, the church of the former abbey, which was returned to the Catholic Church in 1908.

Haussmann had referred to 'the gutting of old Paris' by his new boulevards, and this process was pushed to completion under the Third Republic (1870–1940). Among the works finished was the Opéra, completed in 1875. Designed by Charles Garnier, a largely unknown Parisian who had won an 1861 design competition over about 170 other applicants, its dramatic exterior, which was topped by a roofed cupola, covered a stagey interior that included a 'grand foyer' and a 'grand staircase', ideal sites for social display. The building's skeleton of metal girders provided strength and resistance to fire.

Paris was at the cutting edge of some new developments in culture, science and technology around this time. Its first public cinema was opened in 1895 by the Lumière brothers, and it was the setting for important scientific work by Pasteur and the Curies. Modern-minded Parisians were early adopters of cycling and the internal combustion engine, which would change the shape of urban life in the form of motorcars, buses and lorries.

Elsewhere on the cultural scene, Auguste Rodin's 1879 sculpture *The Call to Arms* was inspired by the defence of the city during the Franco-Prussian War. More of his work can be viewed in the usually crowded but always impressive Musée Rodin, Rue de Varenne. In a similar vein there is a striking monument of a lion at the centre of the Place Denfert-Rochereau, commemorating the defence of the north-eastern city of Belfort by the commander after whom the square is named. The lion is a smaller version of one by Frédéric Auguste Bartholdi, which sits below the castle in Belfort. Bartholdi was also the designer of the Statue of Liberty, of which various smaller replicas exist in Paris; the most prominent of these, donated by the city's American colony, was erected in 1889 on the Île aux Cygnes, a man-made island in the Seine off Passy. Meanwhile, to acknowledge the sense of loss arising from the Franco-Prussian War, a statue representing Strasbourg in the Place de la Concorde was shrouded in mourning fabric.

The establishment of the Third Republic was also marked in Paris statuary, principally by the 1883 monument that still stands in the Place de la République (formerly the Place du Château d'Eau), topped with a bronze figure of Marianne. Relief sculptures around the monument's base depict events in the history of the Republic. So also with the statue *Le Triomphe de la République*, erected in 1899 in the Place de la Nation by Aimé-Jules Dalou.

Alongside this earnest memorialization, tensions were playing out in Paris. In 1887–9 there was a rise in support for General Georges Boulanger, the anti-German Minister of War, who was also anti-republican. He was elected as a deputy for Paris, but did not stage the feared coup; instead, he fled and in 1891 killed himself at the Brussels graveside of his mistress.

The Belle Époque saw the construction of some dramatic buildings with associated statuary, such as the Grand Palais, the Pont Alexandre III and the Orsay railway station. On a smaller scale, elegant steel and glass shopping arcades such as the Galerie Vivienne provided an attractive alternative to the new department stores.

Paris, as ever, was still growing rapidly. As in Britain, the capital was not the centre of coal-based industrialization; however, like London, Paris was a major industrial hub, in part due to the ease with which coal could be moved there by river, canal and rail. Proletarianization was becoming more apparent in the Parisian world of work. Employers were increasingly operating on a large scale, with manufacturing concentrated in factories, and employees consequently found themselves vulnerable. For instance, while cab drivers had for a time been owner-workers or small-scale employers close to their drivers, from 1866 the Compagnie Générale des Voitures played a central role and most drivers became employees. They often went on strike, and industrial action more generally became common from the 1880s onwards. In 1907, the first two women coach drivers appeared. The role of women in the labour force was increasing, even before the major expansion brought about by the First World War.

Some areas became slums, notably the 12th and 13th arrondissements. The high costs and lack of space that characterized life in Paris encouraged many of the poor or modestly off to turn to the suburbs, some of which, such as Bobigny in the north-east, became a 'red belt'. These suburbs offered a different type of slum, a consequence of the poor provision made by the developers. In 1910, the Socialist Party appealed for electoral support there:

> You came to Bobigny fleeing the high rents of Paris and seeking to emancipate yourselves from the rapacity of bourgeois who exploit you in all possible ways. Unfortunately in our city you have found only high taxes, absurdly poor means of communication, rutted streets, insufficient lighting, mounds of garbage, and no drinking water.

There were attractive suburbs, but not the garden interest typical of many residential areas in London. Instead there was a dense inner city, with apartment blocks spreading, and the middle classes still preferred living near the centre. Technological change did, however, improve the potential quality of life in the city, especially when electricity became publicly available from 1875.

Paris's role as a tourist destination was boosted by the accessibility of rail travel. In October 1873, the *Edinburgh Review* commented: 'The enormous extension of Continental travel is one of the great features of the last ten years. During the autumn months the whole of Europe seems to be in a state of perpetual motion.' New hotels were built for all levels of expenditure. Thus, as part of the process through which stations spawned hotels, the Gare d'Orsay was accompanied by the Hôtel d'Orsay, opened in 1897. César Ritz opened his famous hotel in a seventeenth-century building overlooking the Place Vendôme in 1898; it had 210 rooms and included a bathroom in every suite. His junior partner and head chef, Auguste Escoffier, codified much of what is now seen as typical haute cuisine – notably the so-called mother sauces – and sought to impose order on kitchens and codify courses.

Such places were key sites in fictional accounts such as those involving Arsène Lupin, the gentleman burglar created by Maurice Leblanc in 1907. Born and educated in Rouen, Leblanc was typical in having come to Paris to seek his fortune, starting off as a journalist.

A very different figure who came to Paris for similar reasons, and indeed remained there for the rest of his life, was the English fashion designer Charles Frederick Worth. Having moved to the city as a young man in 1846, he became a sales assistant and dress-sewer before establishing a fashion salon in Paris in 1858. From 1860, Napoleon III's wife, the Empress Eugénie, was his most famous client, ensuring that he became a star of the fashion world – by 1898, he was employing 1,200 people. Worth used live models rather than fashion dolls, and made his salon in the Rue de la Paix a social centre; he famously designed a walking skirt and abandoned the impractical crinoline. His fortune enabled him to enjoy a house in the Champs-Élysées and a villa in Suresnes near the Bois de Boulogne. Far less positively, obligatory night work during the busy season and exposure to dangerous chemicals damaged the health of his workers, most of whom were women. From the

The Bonnot gang

WITH CRIME AND REVOLUTION BOTH IN AN ANARCHIST FERMENT,
Paris was the centre for a new type of gang in 1911–12: one
reliant on cars and repeating rifles, that focused on bank
robberies in which cashiers were shot. As the police were largely
reliant on bicycles, the criminals had a major advantage. The
spree ended with a shootout with police at Choisy-le-Roi.

1900s, like many other Parisian workers, their involvement with
unions and strike action increased.

Montmartre had become a centre of artistic activity during
the late nineteenth century. Its cafés, bars and clubs were popular
with local workers and with painters, ensuring that the life of the
district was much reproduced on canvas – notably by Utrillo, Renoir,
Toulouse-Lautrec and, from about 1900, Braque, Vlaminck and
Picasso. The cubist movement owed much to Montmartre, and
there was also innovation in poetry. A key characteristic of Parisian
culture more generally was a willingness to embrace change, and
with it challenges to form and to conventions of representation,
including colour. This bold approach influenced not only visual art
but the design of cars and aircraft, theatre and film sets. Paris was
scarcely alone in this, and indeed in some respects was a European
counterpart to New York.

The Third Republic presided over an uneasy politics and a great
deal of public commemoration, both of which focused on Paris. The
long sequence of regime and constitutional changes that had taken
place since 1792 had led to new public ideologies and accordingly
to new histories, and these were more present in the capital than
anywhere else. It seemed particularly necessary to justify the most

recent changes. Emmanuel Frémiet's gilded bronze equestrian statue of Joan of Arc in the Place des Pyramides, inaugurated in 1874, became a focal point for mass demonstrations by right-wing nationalists, notably in 1896–7 during the Dreyfus affair. Paris was the centre of the affair, both of the alleged treason and of the subsequent controversy, although the retrial in 1899 occurred in Rennes. Alfred Dreyfus, a Jewish officer wrongly convicted in 1894 of spying for the Germans, suffered for and from the antisemitic prejudices of army and society and as a result of the expression of extreme Catholicism. He would eventually be exonerated, but not until 1906. There is a room focusing on the affair in the Museum of Jewish Art and History.

As of 1913, Paris was still Europe's second-largest city behind London – and while both Britain and Germany had more than one city with a population of over a million, this was not the case with France. Paris was also the head of the French empire, both formally and informally, such that the wealth of the French world focused there. Its leading role in culture was seen across all areas

Exhibiting for glorys

TWO OF THE IMPRESSIVE BEAUX-ARTS BUILDINGS BETWEEN THE Champs-Élysées and the Seine were originally constructed as display sites for the Paris Exposition of 1900, which attracted 51 million visitors. Built between 1897 and 1900, the Grand Palais and Petit Palais are both still in use as exhibition spaces. They are masterpieces in iron and glass, part of an impressive late nineteenth-century landscape that also includes the Théâtre du Rond Point, the dramatic single-span Alexander III bridge and the Champs-Élysées gardens.

of the arts, with 1913 marked by the publication of the first section of Marcel Proust's *À la recherche du temps perdu*.

Other great works set in large part in Paris included Guy de Maupassant's *Bel-Ami* (1885), in which Paris is the place where an opportunistic rogue (born in Normandy) manipulates his way to success. Maupassant's description of Paris provides much detail that is necessarily missing from paintings, photographs, and surviving buildings: 'It was one of those summer evenings when Paris is completely without air. The city, hot as an oven, seemed to sweat in the stifling night. The stench of sewage rose from the granite mouths of the sewers, and through the low windows of the basement kitchens, the infamous miasma of washing-up water and old sauces overflowed into the street…passers-by walked past exhausted, hats in hand to cool their foreheads.'

Chapter 11

First World War and
Interwar, 1914–1939

To understand the role of Paris in the twentieth century requires consideration not only of developments in the city itself but of the wider situation in France, and the extent to which both Paris and France were affected by specific international trends and events. Many people tend to think of this period only in terms of the impact of the Second World War but in truth, that is too limited a view. War does, of course, profoundly affect cities – as the situation in Kyiv at the time of writing makes painfully clear – but there are many other factors that contribute to the impact of international developments, and they can sometimes be linked in unexpected ways.

Take the civil unrest in Paris in 1968: it can be, and sometimes is, characterized as an attempted insurrection echoing the themes of the French long nineteenth century. But it also owed much to a more general wave of student and labour activism in which France, to a degree, copied Germany and Italy. Taking an even broader view, one sees that there were long-term cultural trends at play including the increasing global population and the spread of a car culture.

Very soon after war broke out in 1914, Germany attacked Paris. At this point the city had not experienced a bombardment

since 1871, as its wars since then had been imperial. In further-
ance of the Schlieffen Plan, the initial German advance was
designed to encompass Paris as part of an 'envelopment' of the
French army; this would, it was hoped, deliver a rapid victory so
that German troops could switch their attention to the Eastern
Front in order to fight the slower-moving Russian army. The plan,
however, was thwarted by a French response that owed much
to Paris's position as a communications hub. Whereas the
Germans marched forward on foot, French troops travelled
by train from the Lorraine front, where they had launched an
unsuccessful offensive. They then moved forward, some by
Paris buses and taxis, to confront the Germans in the Marne
Valley. Meanwhile, Paris's defences were being organized, with
machine guns for the Eiffel Tower and the large-scale deployment of artillery.

The advance was stopped but the Germans would remain
poised near Paris until the final months of the war, although
their major Western Front offensive in 1915–17, that of 1916, was
directed against Verdun, roughly 140 miles away. For Germany,
the destruction, whether by envelopment or attrition, of the French
army was the priority, rather than the capture of Paris or other
specific locations. The German strategy in 1870 had been essentially the same.

From late August 1914 there were episodes of bombardment by
Zeppelin airships and other aircraft. In March 1918, after a fresh
advance and the deployment of long-range guns, the Germans
were again able to bombard the city, but only at great range and
with a few pieces of heavy artillery. There was significant loss of
life as well as structural damage; a shell hit the church of Saint-
Gervais-Saint-Protais, killing 91 people. The heavy casualties of
the conflict hit Paris very hard – many of its soldiers were killed

or wounded, and the resulting imbalance in numbers of men and women had long-term effects on a generation.

Politics in Paris became more febrile during the war, beginning on 31 July 1914, as the crisis escalated, with the assassination of Jean Jaurès in the Café du Croissant, Rue Montmartre (which still exists). A prominent anti-militarist socialist, Jaurès was seeking to avoid the move toward war, using the language of socialist solidarity. He was shot by Raoul Villain, a nationalist. Villain would eventually be acquitted by a jury, which meant that Jaurès's widow, as plaintiff, had to pay his court costs.

There was an attempt at pro-war solidarity in August 1914 in the form of the Sacred Union, a cross-party agreement to back the war. A patriotic show of support for soldiers departing to the front was rapidly followed by preparations for the German siege, with the government and National Assembly, as a result, moving to Bordeaux and paintings being hastily shifted from the Louvre to Toulouse.

The initial surge of alarm was followed by the heavy and lingering impact of a war economy, all the more crushing because the war lasted far longer than anyone had anticipated. Manufacturing was pushed to a new level of urgency, with new factories built and others repurposed. As so many men, especially young men, were away at the front, the employment of women became commonplace at all levels of society and in many areas of the economy; women's clothing styles were adapted to accommodate the demands of war work, with skirts being shortened.

Inflation was high, coal was in short supply, and there was serious pressure on the standard of living. This led to strikes and serious ministerial instability in 1917 and early 1918, alongside attacks on war profiteering. It was fortunate for the population and the government alike that the war came to an end in 1918.

PARIS MONUMENTAL

MÉTROPOLITAIN

Mata Hari

IT IS TYPICAL, INDEED CLICHÉD, FOR ANY DISCUSSION OF ESPIONAGE to involve a mention of this dancer who became a highly successful courtesan. The Dutch-born Margaretha Zelle (1876–1917), a divorcee, moved to Paris in 1903; she performed first as a circus horse rider and then as an exotic dancer. Recruited as a French spy during the First World War, she was also accused of spying for the Germans. Following her arrest in February 1917, she was convicted of espionage and executed by firing squad in the moat of the Château of Vincennes. Portrayed as a *femme fatale*, she matched the image of the city.

Unlike St Petersburg, Constantinople, Vienna, Budapest and Berlin – all capitals of empires that collapsed as a result of the war – Paris emerged into peacetime without the disruption of a major political transformation and all its attendant socioeconomic chaos. Instead, despite the pressures of demobilization, continuing coal shortages, union radicalism and fiscal problems, postwar Paris was a dynamic city: the capital of one of the victor nations, whose empire had in fact been enlarged by gains in Africa and the Middle East. At the same time, the after-effects of the conflict lingered on in the presence of wounded veterans. The interment of the Unknown Soldier beneath the Arc de Triomphe in 1920 was a major occasion, as had been the previous year's Bastille Day Victory Parade.

The following decade saw not only the 1924 Olympic Games in Paris but also a great flourishing of creativity. France's native artists were joined by many from other countries, including émigrés, such as Russians fleeing communism. This period of movement and artistic innovation was the source for many of the artistic treasures that can be seen in Paris today, including those in the Musée Picasso and some in the museum on Jewish art and history. Jazz and art deco were particularly notable in Paris, as reflected at the 1925 International Exhibition of Decorative and Industrial Arts.

Jazz musicians including Sidney Bechet and Dizzy Gillespie were active in Paris at this time; music-hall stars included the American-born Josephine Baker, Édith Piaf and Mistinguett, whose famous legs were insured for 500,000 francs in 1919. In 2021, decades after her death, Baker became the first black woman to enter the Panthéon, an honour that was once restricted to 'great men' of the Republic. Her remains were not disturbed (she is buried in Monaco); instead, she was represented by a coffin containing handfuls of earth from significant places in her life. In the 1920s Baker had famously performed a *danse sauvage* wearing a string of bananas; later, she worked for the Resistance and supported the civil rights movement.

Fashions were changing; Coco Chanel's influence ushered in an age of more comfortable clothing for women. Avant-garde performances by the Ballets Russes and Ballets Suédois, such as *La Création du monde* (1923), dazzled audiences with boldly designed sets and costumes. Cafés and restaurants served as meeting points for the literary elite; some of these venues remain open today, including Les Deux Magots and the Café de Flore on the Left Bank. They may still be filled with poseurs, but at today's prices they are far less accessible to impoverished writers.

The interwar period also saw Montparnasse become increasingly popular with radical artists, replacing the more expensive Montmartre in that role. Many of the artists living there were foreign-born, including Modigliani, Chagall and Soutine, but there was also an important Parisian cohort. The energy continued until the Second World War. Popular Montparnasse venues that still survive include La Rotonde, opened in 1903; Le Dôme (1906); and La Coupole (1927) – although none of these now plays the same sort of role as in the 1920s and '30s, when F. Scott Fitzgerald and Ernest Hemingway were part of the milieu.

The Blue Train

THE YEAR 1922 SAW NEW 'BLUE TRAINS' APPEAR ON THE THROUGH run from Calais via Paris to the Côte d'Azur of the French Riviera. These were an important part of the postwar programme of the International Sleeping Car Company.

Previously, sleeping cars had been constructed with a framework of wood resting upon a chassis of metal; but in the new cars, wood was only used for interior decoration and the framework, partitions, ceiling and floor were made of steel. Earlier sleeping cars had two or four berths per compartment, while the 1922 trains had single-berth compartment coaches – each taking sixteen passengers, as formerly, but with the total length increased. Paris was the starting point for long-range services including the Orient Express; the first direct train to Constantinople (Istanbul) left Paris in 1889, while the opening of the Simplon Tunnel enabled a more southerly rail route. The romance of international travel was related to that of Paris, and vice versa.

The postwar city attracted a steady stream of foreign visitors including large numbers of Americans, many of whom settled there. In 1919, Sylvia Beach opened Shakespeare and Company, a bookshop that became a landmark meeting place for expats including Hemingway and Ezra Pound. The twenty-year-old American John Dickson Carr spent five months in Europe, most of that time in Paris, and its influence is evident in his first detective novel, *It Walks By Night* (1930). Set in 1927, evoking luxury and mystery, it presents 'the revolving jewel of Paris – lights and shadows, perfume and danger – the *salon*, the greenroom, the pits-abbey, brothel, and guillotine, a Babylonian carnival…' Agatha Christie's *Mystery of the Blue Train* (1928) also makes Paris a setting for criminal activity, opening with an unsuccessful mugging by 'apaches' (thugs).

The police in Paris could be brutal and corrupt as well as incompetent and politically partisan, the latter a characteristic they shared with the magistracy. From 1927 to 1934, the Prefect of Paris, Jean Chiappe, was both the protégé of the Minister of the Interior and steeped in criminality. Among other activities, he assisted the notorious fraudster Alexandre Stavisky, who eventually died from a gunshot wound, having either taken his own life or been murdered by the police. Revelations led to the resignation of the prime minister, Camille Chautemps. His replacement, Édouard Daladier, dismissed Chiappe. The upshot of all this was a far-right riot in the Place de la Concorde in 1934 that led to the police killing fifteen rioters, resulting in the fall of the new government. Violence was not uncommon in connection with political meetings, as different parties sought to control, intimidate and protect themselves in public spaces. Thus, in Clichy in 1937, a left-wing demonstration against a right-wing cinema evening ended in police action followed by vicious street fighting.

Paris also continued to be a site for the inscription of lessons from the past. In 1936, at a time when the Popular Front government appeared to be under attack from the right, a demonstration took place to commemorate those killed in the suppression of the Commune in 1871. It included posters depicting other heroes of the French past who could be appropriated by the left.

The classic detective

PIETR-LE-LETTON, THE FIRST OF GEORGES SIMENON'S MAIGRET novels, was published in 1931. The Commissioner of the Paris Brigade Criminelle became not only the most famous French detective in the course of seventy-five novels, twenty-eight short stories, and numerous film, TV radio adaptations, but also a guide to Paris and Parisian life. Sixty-three of the novels were set in the city, where he worked at 36 Quai des Orfèvres. Maigret was based on Marcel Guillaume, a commissioner of note with whom Simenon was acquainted. The first story moves from a body at the Gare du Nord to the Hotel Majestic and then back to Maigret's office, all set against a background of rain and succinct description.

Simenon lived in various different parts of Paris, including Batignolles (near Montmartre) and the Place des Vosges; while Maigret lived in the Boulevard Richard-Lenoir near the Canal Saint-Martin, from which part of a corpse was to be recovered in *Maigret et le corps sans tête* (1955). On a murky evening, the canal still conveys menace.

The 1930s saw the strains of the Great Depression exacerbate political differences, with worker militancy a particular issue in the middle of the decade. There were persistent problems for France (more so than in Britain) in regaining the economic activity of the 1920s, and the gold standard for the franc had to be abandoned in 1936. Nevertheless, in Paris there was also much prosperity and elegance as well as new building – although, in a contrast with London, far too little new housing. This left a legacy of inadequate housing for post-1945 governments, greatly affecting the health of the poorest in society for decades to come.

As in London, prosperity was linked to dynamic sectors of the economy such as car manufacture – France was Europe's top producer until it was surpassed by Britain in 1933 – and white goods. Renault's main factory, located on the Île Seguin at Billancourt in Paris's western suburbs, eventually became the largest in the country. Paris was relatively little affected by the decline in traditional heavy industry such as iron and steel, shipbuilding and related engineering. Additionally, the state continued to be a major source of employment.

Citroën

ANDRÉ CITROËN, A FORMER ARMS MANUFACTURER, FOUNDED his car company in 1919, with the first Citroën Type A being produced that year at a factory on the Quai de Javel (now the Quai André-Citroën). It was exhibited in a showroom at 43 Champs-Élysées, which is still in use by Citroën today.

From 1925 to 1934 the Eiffel Tower was brightly illuminated with the company's name, serving as 'the world's largest advertisement'. This arrangement ended when the company went bankrupt. Although it was refinanced by Michelin, the change in fortune allowed Renault to regain its former position as France's most successful carmaker.

Wealth generation in the Paris area was matched by the city's continuing role as a centre of conspicuous consumption, which in turn provided jobs. Rich foreign visitors might be fewer in number these days, but they still came: Paris remained a prime destination, especially for Americans and Britons, right up until the German conquest in June 1940. Indeed, that March, 'Chips' Channon, a British MP who knew Paris well, wrote in his diary: 'Paris is gayer and more lit up by night than is London,' adding on 1 April: 'I wandered about Paris, beautiful, so tantalising: the shops are more fascinating than ever and there is little sign of war except the absence of buses.'

Like Berlin and London, Paris had an active sex scene – as Channon, who was bisexual and rather promiscuous, knew well. Alongside being the national, if not global, centre of prostitution, it was notorious for decadent clubs like the Sphynx in the Place Pigalle. Earlier, as the Nouvelle Athens, this had been a café patronized by artists; it eventually became the New Moon, which by the 1970s was a rock musicians' haunt.

Sous les toits de Paris
(Under the Roofs of Paris)

DIRECTED BY RENÉ CLAIR, THIS 1930 MUSICAL COMEDY HAD A MAJOR impact as the first French film of the sound era to become a legitimate international hit. It was filmed on a studio set depicting a street of Paris tenements, and tells a story of love and jealousy amidst a semi-criminal milieu in a lively working-class neighbourhood. Its influence on a genre of French cinema is undeniable.

Airports for Paris

PARIS'S FIRST AIRPORT, LE BOURGET, OPENED COMMERCIAL
operations in 1919, with flights to and from London particularly
important. Orly, in turn, was opened in 1932. Regular
commercial traffic at Le Bourget ceased in 1980, but the airport
remains important for business flights and also houses the
French air and space museum.

Orly served as the city's main airport from 1952, when
Air France transferred all its operations there from Le Bourget,
until Charles de Gaulle opened in 1974. Orly has three runways
and remains a significant passenger airport, although it is poorly
connected to the centre of Paris.

Paris became not only the principal production centre of French
cinema, but a popular subject for classic films like 1938's *Hôtel du
Nord*, set on the Canal Saint-Martin: a strongly etched, well-acted
working-class drama in which poverty, crime and sex intersect in
such a way that murder is almost inevitable.

Notable new buildings from the 1920s included Le Corbusier's
Villa La Roche and Villa Jeanneret in Auteuil; now combined into
the Fondation Le Corbusier, they showcase his use of white concrete
and embrace of light. The following decade saw the construction
of the Palais de Chaillot, built for the 1937 World's Fair: a prominent right-bank counterpoint to the Eiffel Tower, it is dramatically
neoclassical in style with sweeping curves and columns, opening
out to the Trocadéro gardens and fountains that are the setting
for modern sculptures such as Daniel Bacqué's *Woman*. The site
also incorporated museums, a theatre and a cinema. Its spirit
was provided by Raoul Dufy's mural *The Spirit of Electricity* – a

reminder that part of the modernization of this period was provided by an extensive electrification programme, reducing the need for smoking chimneys with their corrosive effects. This change was also reflected in the appearance of electric trains to serve some destinations from Paris.

The divisions of the interwar years heralded the radicalization that would contribute to the collapse of the Third Republic in 1940 and its replacement by Vichy. Yet there was no earlier equivalent to the fall of Weimar Germany in 1933, and democracy held on until 1940, as it did not do in most of Continental Europe.

Chapter 12

Second World War, 1939–1945

Preparation for war with Germany gathered pace from February 1939, initially with the construction of bomb shelters. The distribution of gas masks followed in March, when Hitler broke the Munich agreement. At the end of August, as the crisis over Poland gathered pace, children and artistic treasures were evacuated, street lights switched off and buildings protected by sandbags. Rationing followed, while many Parisians were called up.

Launched on 10 May 1940, the German offensive on the Western Front was rapidly successful. Paris was hit by bombing from 3 June, with 254 people killed that day, and the government left a week later – as did much of the population in a panic-flight from the city, using any available means of transport.

Rather than emulating the Communards, the French government declared on the 12th that there would be no resistance in the city. This spared Paris the fate of Warsaw when conquered by Germany in 1939. The Germans accordingly occupied the city on the 14th and Hitler inspected it ten days later; he was particularly impressed by Napoleon's tomb. This would be his only visit to Paris (see plate XV).

While Vichy operated as an alternative capital – that of the unoccupied zone – Paris effectively became a German city with its principal buildings housing German agencies. The Palais Bourbon, for example, became the headquarters of the military administration instead of the National Assembly. Benefiting from a manipulated exchange rate, German military personnel treated the city as a tourist destination. Street signs were now in German, as were the clocks – Berlin time became public time. Brothels, hotels and restaurants adapted to their new circumstances. Many of those who had fled the city gradually returned, while the Nazi–Soviet pact of 1939 led to cooperation from the Communist Party.

Paris was a centre of industrial production as well as leisure for the Germans, but for loyal Parisians (as opposed to the many who collaborated) the occupation was a time of great difficulty. Even with rationing there were frequent shortages of coal and food, much of which was appropriated by the Germans; people began to use their balconies and local parks for growing food and keeping animals. Apartments were requisitioned and Germans travelled free on the Métro. Queues became ubiquitous. A black market developed alongside serious poverty and misery even as, for the well-connected few, the good life continued largely uninterrupted.

The consequences included an increased death rate and a significant rise in diseases such as tuberculosis. Malnutrition meant children suffered from rickets and stunted growth. There was a harshly enforced curfew as well as arbitrary arrests, searches and street closures. The German authorities and the police were assisted by collaborators including criminals freed from prison, many of whom acquired considerable influence within the occupying regime. The Vichy government was itself a form of collaboration directed against the republican tradition and metropolitan culture of Paris.

Pariser

LEVALLOIS

NEUILLY

BOIS DE BOULOGNE

ISSY

VANVES

MONTROUGE

lan

Das Geschichtliche und Kunsthistorische ~ Paris ~

1. — Louvre Palast.
2. — Triumphbogen Carrousel.
3. — Pl. de la Concorde - Obelisk.
4. — Grand Palais.
5. — Etoile. Triumphbogen mit dem Grab des Unbekannten Soldaten.
6. — Chaillot Palast.
7. — Eiffelturm.
8. — Militær Schule.
9. — Dôme des Invalides.
10. — Abgeordneten Haus (franzœsische Kammer).
11. — St-Germain-des-Prés Kirche.
12. — Franzœsische Akademie.
13. — Luxembourg Palast (Senat).
14. — Cluny.
15. — Panthéon.
16. — Moschee.
17. — Notre-Dame.
18. — Hl. Kapelle.
19. — St-Jakobsturm.
20. — Rathaus.
21. — Vendôme. Platz mit Sæule.
22. — Hl. Magdalena Kirche.
23. — Opernhaus.
24. — Bœrse.
25. — Augustinus Kirche.
26. — Hl. Herz Jesu Kirche.
27. — Tor Saint-Denis.
28. — Tor Saint-Martin.
29. — Statue der Republique.
30. — Bastille Platz mit Gedænksæule.
31. — Nation Platz.
32. — Park Buttes-Chaumont.
33. — Lœwe von Belfort.

PANTIN

LE PRÉ SAINT-GERVAIS

BOIS DE VINCENNES

CHARENTON

IVRY

Coco Chanel

THE PASSAGE OF TIME CAN CHANGE THE REPUTATION OF FAMOUS Parisians. Collaboration or compliance with German occupiers has tarnished the legacies of such famous figures as the singer Maurice Chevalier and the philosopher Jean-Paul Sartre; so, too, the talented clothes designer Coco Chanel (1883–1971), better known for her comfortable but still elegant clothes and for her signature scent.

Chanel's collaboration with the Germans ranged from sexual liaisons to antisemitic despoilation of her Jewish competitors. Having worked for two different branches of German intelligence, she thought it prudent to move to Switzerland in 1945. After the war, while Christian Dior became an international sensation in 1947 with his feminine 'New Look', Chanel did not present a comeback collection until 1954. She died in the Ritz, where she had spent most of the war alongside her German friends, and her funeral was held in the Madeleine.

There were signs of opposition. On 11 November 1940, Parisian students demonstrated against the decision taken by the German authorities and the collaborationist prefecture of Paris to downplay the commemoration of the Armistice ending the First World War. This demonstration was violently suppressed, and is commemorated with a plaque at the Arc de Triomphe unveiled by President Sarkozy in 2010.

The situation was particularly difficult for Jews, who were barred from most occupations in October 1940. They were forced to wear yellow stars, and Jewish sites were vandalized. In July

1942, more than 13,000 non-French Jews were rounded up in Paris and its suburbs and held in internment camps, including at Drancy in north-eastern Paris. About 10,000 of them were sent to Auschwitz between 17 July and 31 August including, in the first transport, children. The extent to which these deportations were handled by the French authorities, who indeed controlled Drancy in 1942, was concealed after the end of the war. In 1943–4, French Jews were rounded up, again by French police, for deportation to slaughter, again with the French authorities playing a major role. This was not mentioned when the Memorial to the Martyrs of the Deportation was inaugurated in Paris in 1962 by Charles de Gaulle.

Sensitivity to France's role increased from the late 1970s. In 1993 René Bousquet, who had served as chief of police in the occupied zone of France from 1942, was assassinated in Paris just before he could be tried for his role in rounding up Jewish children for slaughter in Germany. This directed attention onto his friend François Mitterrand, who had been France's president since 1981.

The memorialization of the Holocaust gathered pace under Mitterrand's long-time opponent Jacques Chirac, mayor of Paris from 1977, who succeeded him as president in 1995 and remained in office until 2007. Plaques were erected at Parisian schools about the wartime seizure of Jewish pupils for slaughter, and the Holocaust Memorial, an impressive museum and memorial in the 4th arrondissement, was opened by Chirac in Paris in 2005. In a high-profile 2007 ceremony at the Panthéon, Chirac honoured the Righteous of France, those who had helped Jews during the German occupation. His successors in office continued to emphasize the issue; in 2012, François Hollande gave a speech reiterating that the Holocaust had taken place 'in our capital, in our streets...on our school playgrounds'.

Resistance activity had gathered pace from August 1941, with the German attack on the Soviet Union in June having prompted communists to become active in the Resistance. Attacks became more common from early 1943, leading to German pressure on the French police who deployed Brigades Spéciales. Resistance was harshly punished with mass executions and the frequent use of torture in order to identify and destroy networks. What can be described as the German 'murder of the future' included shooting pupils who demonstrated in favour of their arrested teachers. Many such deaths are commemorated by plaques in the city today, and executed Resistance fighters are commemorated in Division 97 of the Père-Lachaise.

In August 1944, in response to the progress of Allied operations in Normandy, the Resistance rose, supported by much of the Paris police. Fighting in the boulevards, in which about 800 to 1,000 members of the Resistance were killed, gave an idea of what could have happened in 1940 if there had been resistance at that point to the German occupation. The uprising caused some damage to buildings including the Palais Bourbon, and to this day the bullet holes that remain serve as a pointed reminder of the fighting. Advancing Free French troops joined with the Resistance to liberate Paris, with Philippe Leclerc's Second French Armoured Division playing a key role. The theme of liberation by the French was to be important to France's postwar recovery of its national identity, although the entire context had been set by the Allied invasion of France on D-Day and the subsequent battle in Normandy.

The decision by the German commander to ignore Hitler's demands that Paris be destroyed was significant. It meant that there was no equivalent damage in the city to that inflicted at the château at Vincennes by the Germans before they retreated, nor to the sabotage by the Germans as part of their hard-fought defence at Cherbourg. Instead, Paris became a theatre of political rebirth by and for Charles de Gaulle, leader of the Free French, who became head of the new Provisional Government of the French Republic.

After liberation the Germans began to rain down bombs and rockets on the city, killing many. At the same time, collaborators were arrested and some executed. The final year of the war saw the stabilization of the new French government, which helped ensure only a limited role for the Allies. Liberation brought freedom, if not plenty – as the lawyer Maurice Garçon noted in his diary: 'Everything is lacking. No wood, no coal, no electricity and almost no gas.'

In the aftermath of the conflict there was a stain on the reputation of various prominent Parisians known to have collaborated or complied, including Coco Chanel and Jean-Paul Sartre. The Resistance was memorialized in the Flame of Liberty at the northern end of the Pont de l'Alma, and the efforts of the Free French forces inspired the rechristening of the bridge now known as the Pont de Bir-Hakeim, with its accompanying statue by Holger Wederkinch. To mark France's wartime alliance with the Soviet Union, the Place de Stalingrad (subsequently renamed the Place de la Bataille-de-Stalingrad) was created in 1945 from what had been part of the Boulevard de la Villette.

Visitors to the city today can learn more at the Musée de l'Ordre de la Libération in the Invalides, and the General Leclerc and Jean Moulin museum in the Place Denfert-Rochereau (14th arrondissement) provides much information on both Resistance and Liberation.

Chapter 13

Postwar Developments, 1945–1981

A host of modern structures capture the dynamism of postwar Paris, from the Centre Georges Pompidou in the city centre to La Défense (see plate XVIII) and the Stade de France in the inner suburbs. This energy, which captivates tourists, has developed against an ever-changing political, social and economic backdrop over the past eight decades. The Paris of 1945, suffering in the aftermath of a brutal occupation, was not the same as that of 1973 following a period of vertiginous economic growth; and the more varied fortunes of recent decades have seen the city continue to evolve.

In economic terms, Paris was able to function successfully after 1945 within the context of a broader Western economic recovery, followed by a boom period that lasted for nearly thirty years. The boom times returned, albeit in a more subdued and episodic fashion, from the 1980s until the late 2000s, with the lower growth rates of this later period lending a different tone to politics.

As such, Paris was in some ways an outlier of American and (West) German prosperity and activity, able to retain its status as a world city without being constrained by the French economic system. There was a parallel to the earlier benefits stemming from French imperialism, including the 'informal empire' seen in Latin

America. The effects of this prosperity were particularly evident in central Paris, but also more generally across the city. It is not insignificant that the first tower to open in the business district of La Défense, in 1964, was named after an American company – the Esso building. America's role in Paris had changed greatly since the beginning of the First World War.

Initially in the aftermath of Second World War, things looked far less promising. Rationing continued, as did the grave crisis in both quantity and quality of housing. The Allied bombing of factories in the suburbs, notably Billancourt, had lasting effects. There was also a partial reckoning with collaborators, the return of those forced to work in wartime Germany, and the strain of establishing a new constitution – all taking place in the looming shadow of the Cold War. The flexing of muscles by the communists in 1947 did not lead to the feared general strike but did increase tension, particularly in Paris. Socially and politically divided, the city had voted in the Rassemblement du Peuple Français, de Gaulle's political movement, in that year's municipal elections.

Other new movements of the period included Emmaus, a charity launched by the Abbé Pierre in 1949 from a derelict house in Neuilly that he repaired in order to help the homeless. His call for help on Radio Luxembourg, published in *Le Figaro* during the very cold winter of 1954, was a reminder of the difficulty of the period and of the strength of Catholic communalism:

> A woman froze to death tonight at 3.00 a.m. on the pavement of Sebastopol Boulevard, clutching the eviction notice which the day before had made her homeless…in the last three hours, two aid centres have been created…they are already overflowing, we must open them everywhere.

'Chips' Channon as tourist

THE US-BORN BRITISH POLITICIAN HENRY 'CHIPS' CHANNON (1897–1958) was a passionate Europhile who recorded his impressions of Paris in his extensive diaries, posthumously published to much acclaim.

Channon visited Paris frequently throughout his life and saw the city as elegant and luxurious, the women were 'superbly dressed' and the inhabitants lived a 'super-civilised existence'. During a visit in May 1946, Channon noted how Paris had recovered quickly from the damage caused by the Second World War and described the luxury and beauty of Parisian shops, viewing their frivolous fineries as something post-war London was sorely lacking.

However, Channon was far less complementary towards Paris while visiting in June 1952, describing the French he encountered as 'bad-mannered…filthy Frogs, smelly stingy and rude'. Nevertheless, Paris was soon back in favour after he attended a dinner and ball with a beautiful Parisian dressed head-to-toe in Dior: 'the elegance here enough to make me like Paris'.

The 1950s and 1960s also saw a new flourishing of the Parisian literary scene, often playing out in some of the same cafés that had been cultural hotspots between the wars. The Left Bank was the centre of an intellectual world that offered an important alternative to American-inflected popular culture. The influence of radical thinkers contributed to a sense of flux and a tendency to view established norms and values as no more than passing conventions. Structuralism, a movement that looked in particular

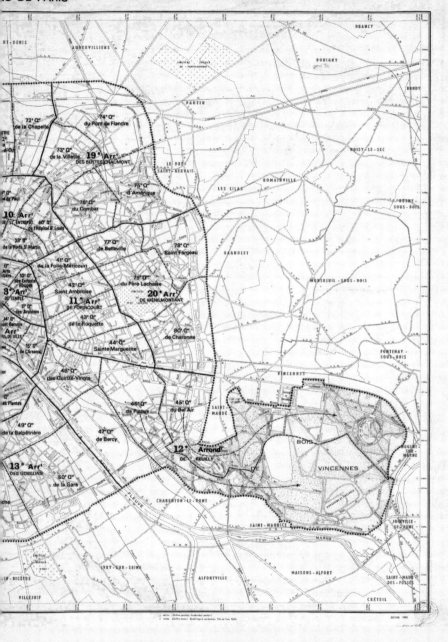

to Claude Lévi-Strauss and Roland Barthes, treated language as a set of concepts that were themselves of limited value as guides to any underlying reality. Although links (like definitions) were far from clear-cut, this situation anticipated postmodernism, which would become influential in the 1980s.

Existentialism, a nihilistic philosophical movement closely associated with thinkers such as Jean-Paul Sartre, Albert Camus and Simone de Beauvoir, stressed the vulnerability of the individual in a hostile world and the emptiness, and thus delusion, of choice. This approach resonated with the non-realist 'theatre of the absurd' of Samuel Beckett and Eugène Ionesco, both of whom settled in Paris. Public intellectuals like Sartre, Jacques Derrida and Michel Foucault developed a worldwide reputation and were more than passing visitors to the city. Having arrived aged twenty to study, Foucault remained there for much of 1946–52 and 1961–84. Foreign writers and philosophers also continued to gravitate to Paris, including James Baldwin, a major American Black intellectual who settled there in 1948 and stayed until his death in 1987.

A prominent new building of this period, and one that represented both France's international significance and the extent to which Paris still welcomed important new architectural projects, was the Maison de l'UNESCO (1958). While the building itself has only limited charm, its decoration and plentiful statuary, including Henry Moore's *Reclining Figure*, are of great interest.

Also in 1958 came the beginning of the 35-kilometre-long (22 miles) Boulevard Périphérique: a ring road around the city, mostly at its administrative boundary. This rapidly successful road, completed in 1973, was more urban motorway than boulevard. It soon became congested, leading to the construction of the more outlying A86 autoroute, which was finished in 2011;

x, Located in the 5th arrondissement of Paris, the Panthéon was designed by Jacques-Germain
Soufflot and built between 1758 and 1798. Originally intended to be a church dedicated
to Saint Geneviève, in 1791 the National Constituent Assembly voted for it to become a
mausoleum for distinguished French citizens.

XI, *The Storming of the Bastille* by Henry Singleton, *c.* 1789–91. On 14 July 1789 revolutionary insurgents attempted to seize the Bastille. After much fighting the governor allowed the revolutionaries to enter and take control of the Bastille.

XII, ABOVE The Eiffel Tower under construction, photographed by Theophile Feau, 1887–8. It stands 320 metres high (1,050 feet) and is one of the most famous monuments in France. It was designed by the engineer Gustave Eiffel between 1887 and 1889.

XIII, OPPOSITE ABOVE *Bal du moulin de la Galette* by Pierre-Auguste Renoir, 1876. The painting depicts a Sunday afternoon at the Moulin de la Galette in Montmartre, where Parisians would dance, drink and eat galettes.

XIV, OPPOSITE BELOW *Avenue de l'Opéra: Morning Sunshine* by Camille Pissarro, 1898. The view of the Avenue de l'Opéra was painted by Pissarro while he was living in the Grand Hôtel du Louvre; in total he painted fifteen views from the hotel.

xv, ABOVE Adolf Hitler in Paris, June 1940, with the Eiffel Tower in the background. Paris was occupied by German forces on 13 June 1940 and Hitler visited Paris the day after France signed the armistice.

XVI, TOP Student demonstrations in May 1968. The civil unrest lasted seven weeks and led to widespread disruption across the country, with many fearing another revolution.

XVII, ABOVE On 15 April 2019, just before 6.20 p.m., a fire broke out in the roof of Notre-Dame Cathedral. The fire caused the cathedral's spire to collapse completely and the majority of the roof was destroyed.

PARiS 2024

XVIII, TOP La Grande Arche de la Défense in the business district of La Défense was part of the Grands Projets of François Mitterrand to introduce more modern monuments in Paris. Construction began in 1985 and was completed in 1989 by the Danish architect Johan Otto von Spreckelsen and engineer Erik Reitzel.

XIX, ABOVE The 2024 Paris Olympics logo, described as the 'face' of the games, combines the Olympic flame, the gold medal and Marianne, the national personification of the French Republic.

Telling the time – or not

DURING AN EARLY SCHOOLBOY VISIT TO PARIS I FOUND MYSELF
walking back to the hotel on my own. Near the back of the Élysée,
a smart car drew up and I was asked (as I translated) if I had the
time. After consulting my watch I got the answer correct in my
best schoolboy French, only to be greeted with an incredulous
shake of the head from the lady within, who drove off.

Years later, while doing archival research in the city, I took
a stroll near the Bastille only to discover my watch had stopped.
There were several vans of CRS deployed, but having looked
at the black-clad riot police ready for action against a nearby
demonstration, I thought it prudent not to ask.

and then, even further out, the Francilienne, begun in 1970 but
still incomplete. The Périphérique is a prominent example of a
kind of motorized Haussmannism that characterized much of
the planning in mid-twentieth-century Paris, curbed only by the
serious economic downturn of the 1970s. Roads and road tunnels
were driven through along the Right Bank of the Seine, altering
pedestrian access to the river, but plans for similar work on the
Left Bank and for a major north–south road were rejected by
Valéry Giscard d'Estaing after he became president in 1974. The
downturn also contributed to a new emphasis on conservation.

Commuting had become more significant to the lives of ordinary people as many residents of Paris moved out towards the
suburbs. The population of the city was to fall from 2.75 million
in 1962 to 2.15 million in 1992, and that despite immigration,
particularly from French North Africa, Spain, Italy and Portugal.
In part, the migration to the suburbs reflected the spread of office

James Bond in Paris

'FROM A VIEW TO A KILL', A SHORT STORY IN *FIVE SECRET OCCASIONS*
in the Life of James Bond (1960), offers a jaundiced view of
Paris and its people that is not really essential to the story; it
presumably reflects Ian Fleming's personal ire and the crises
of the Fourth Republic. The city is presented as having sold
its heart not only to tourists, but to Russians and Romanians.
Should Bond bother to look for a girl, he reflects, she will no
doubt prove disappointing despite outward appearances, using
careful make-up and clothing to conceal bad skin, undyed roots
and a poor figure.

The condescension of Fleming's disgusted attack on the
deception of French beauty seems to reflect a fear of being
deceived. There is also an implicit contrast with the admirable
qualities of British women, drawing upon a long tradition of
British adventure stories.

buildings in the city centre, but it was also a response to people's
desire for more space, including room to park a car. Some of the
suburban construction that took place at this time was high-rise
public housing, which, as with similar building projects in Paris,
was seen as an answer to the protracted and still severe housing
crisis. This had its origins in a lack of sufficient new building
during the interwar period, wartime damage and lack of repair,
and the need to replace poor housing stock. Housing those fleeing
imperial failure in Indochina (principally Vietnam) and Algeria
was an additional task – again, one largely pushed out to the
suburbs, where new satellite towns sprang up, but also into the
poorer outlying arrondissements such as the 15th. There were

also problems with the inherited industrial capability, much of which was unmodernized.

Alongside long-term economic growth and modernization, there were inevitable political and economic tensions. The Algerian crisis of the late 1950s and early '60s led to violence: Algerian demonstrators were killed by the Paris police in 1961, with some bodies being thrown into the Seine. This atrocity was hushed up and has only come under appropriate scrutiny in recent years. Earlier in 1961, an extremist terrorist group of French settlers in Algeria had carried out a bomb attack on the Paris–Strasbourg train.

Student activism in 1967, which reflected the strain on existing academic facilities, practices and hierarchies posed by growing student numbers and a shift towards radicalism, was followed in May 1968 by demonstrations and violence in the capital (see plate XVI). A brutal response by riot police led to a consolidation of support around the students, including a general strike followed by more sustained trade-union action and political pressure from the left for governmental change. Having been assured on 29 May, as a result of a visit to the commanders of the French forces in West Germany, of military support if necessary, de Gaulle then showed determination in a radio broadcast on 30 May. This helped him to regain the initiative, encouraged by a mass demonstration on the same day by his supporters in Paris. On 23 and 24 June de Gaulle's followers won an overwhelming majority in legislative elections, while the left did badly. The students' movement subsequently collapsed as a result of internal divisions and declining popular support.

Events in Paris were often interpreted in the light of the city's historical background; thus, the left saw echoes of the French Revolution in the *événements de mai* 1968, when left-wing popular action challenged the state on the streets of Paris. Such references made their way into literature and cinema over the following decades, such as the 2005 film *Les Amants réguliers*.

Another basis for radical action, the position of the workers, was weakened by deindustrialization. This change is reflected in the presence of new facilities on old industrial sites, such as the Parc André Citroën in the 15th arrondissement – a public green space built on the site of a large Citroën car factory that shut down in the 1970s. There is a similar history behind the Parc de la Villette, with its complex of cultural venues that replaced enormous nineteenth-century abattoirs at La Villette in north-east Paris.

Somewhat differently, the city's existing train system was trans-formed in the 1970s by the development of a major underground transit hub at Châtelet-Les Halles, which opened in 1977 and became the central point of the Parisian rail system. Changes like this were part of a 'new Paris', fundamentally changing the way residents experienced the city, even if tourists were still rather lulled by earlier versions of the cityscape. The fact that Châtelet-Les Halles was underground contributed another element to this contrast between the newly reinvented aspects of Paris and the still-vibrant reminders of its past.

Chapter 14

From Mitterrand to the Present, 1981–2023

Despite much talk of devolution in government, Paris became more connected than ever to the rest of France with the launch of high-speed TGV (*Train à Grande Vitesse*) trains in the early 1980s, strengthening the significance of rail to the city and providing a good alternative to domestic air services. The arrival of the TGVs led many wealthy Parisians to acquire second homes in attractive older quarters such as Avignon and Aix, furthering a socially divisive process of regeneration in poor areas of the city and the surrounding countryside. The TGV services operated out of existing stations, rather than new ones being built.

Alongside the longer-term restoration of old buildings and districts, notably the Marais and the 7th arrondissement, Paris saw a fresh injection of energy into its programme of public development under François Mitterrand, the Socialist president from 1981 to 1995. Mitterrand set in motion a number of costly *grands projets* in the city, including a new national library, the 'People's Opera' at the Bastille and the Grande Arche at La Défense. These works were presented as a justification of the government and an opportunity to advance its views. As the bicentenary of the Revolution, 1989 proved an important year for some of them to open, including the Opéra, the Arche and the new pyramid entrance to the Louvre. Public memorialization and reflection on the Revolution was widespread in the form of ceremonies and conferences, and stickers appeared on lampposts decrying its consequences in the Vendée as genocide.

The Grande Arche, incorporating an exhibition centre as well as a library, was described as a modern counterpart to the Arc de Triomphe inspired by humanitarian ideals rather than war. Strictly speaking it is more of an open cube than an arch, and is larger than Notre-Dame. La Défense itself is an extraordinary area of once cutting-edge architecture supported by sculptures and other works of public art. Many of its buildings have aged well, and it is worth the visitor's time to explore – it also offers excellent views across Paris, towards the Louvre.

Another late twentieth-century improvement to the city that can readily be enjoyed by tourists is the Promenade Plantée. This elevated linear park with workshops and cafés underneath occupies the disused Paris to Vincennes railway line that was abandoned in 1969. Since opening in the early 1990s it has served as an inspiration for similar urban projects elsewhere in the world, including New York City's High Line.

President Chirac continued his predecessor's munificence at the expense of French society as a whole, opening in 2006 what became the Musée du Quai Branly-Jacques Chirac: a museum focusing on the art and culture of Indigenous and colonized peoples, housed in a distinctly modern stilt-borne building designed by Jean Nouvel. Nouvel's other works in Paris include the Arab World Institute, the Cartier Foundation for Contemporary Art and the Philharmonie, a major concert hall in the Parc de la Villette that opened in 2015 (having cost 386 million euros rather than the anticipated 170 million). Although the Musée du Quai Branly-Jacques Chirac is less famous than the Centre Georges Pompidou and the Musée

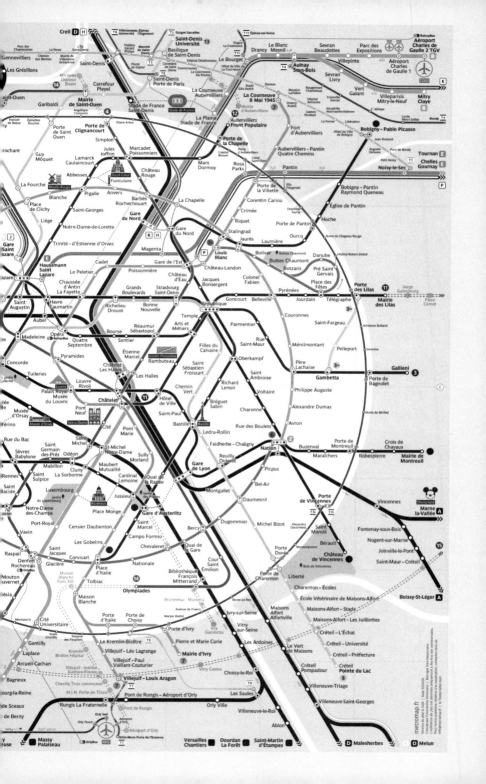

To burger or not

IN THE 1990S THERE WAS OPPOSITION TO MCDONALD'S IN PARIS, while in 2023 plans for a Burger King in Martin Nardaud Square, in the 20th arrondissement near Père Lachaise Cemetery, led to protest – as did plans for another in Châtillon.

Despite concerns about noise, litter and a general lowering of the tone, it's clear that not all Parisians are unwilling to spend their money on ultra-processed burgers and fried chicken. Over the decade from 2011 to 2021 the number of fast-food outlets in the capital grew by 50 per cent to approximately 3,000, while in 2023 the Popeyes Louisiana Kitchen chain opened its first French branch opposite the Gare du Nord.

d'Orsay – which were the presidential projects of Pompidou and Valéry Giscard d'Estaing respectively – it too is well worth visiting. Architecturally it is more impressive at close quarters than it might appear from a distance, in part because there was opposition to the idea of the museum dominating nearby buildings. Since its opening, there has been controversy over whether some of its holdings ought to be returned to their places of origin.

Such works did not resonate with all Parisians. In the poor, immigrant-dense suburbs, especially Grigny, there were riots in 2005 and again in 2007 that involved the torching of thousands of cars. These events provided the politician Nicolas Sarkozy, born and educated in Paris, with an opportunity to display his toughness. As Minister of the Interior in 2005–7, his criticism of the supposed negative effects of immigration and Islamism was met with counter-arguments that social exclusion, and the resulting very high rate of youth unemployment, were the real key issues

– but even so, the points he made seemed to resonate with many voters. His popularity rose, and in 2007 he was elected president. Reforms under Sarkozy's leadership led to opposition in the form of strikes, and from 2008 the government was in increasing difficulty. Some of the challenging issues with which Parisian society was grappling at this time were reflected in the themes of the television drama *Engrenages* (*Spiral*, 2005–20), a police procedural set in a very rough part of the capital.

In 2012, Sarkozy lost the presidential election to François Hollande – but he too faced rising unpopularity, in part because of the country's ongoing economic difficulties. Islamist terrorist attacks in 2015, including the infamous *Charlie Hebdo* attack in January and the Bataclan theatre attack in November, prompted a robust government response involving the deployment of troops. Seventeen people died as a consequence of the January attacks, and 130 more in November. The crisis was stilled, but it had underlined the vulnerability of city life. Hollande did not stand again in 2017, and he was succeeded by Emmanuel Macron.

A very different type of challenge faced Parisians on the evening of 15 April 2019, when the world looked on in horror as Notre-Dame Cathedral caught fire (see plate XVII). The flames quickly spread to the cathedral's ribbed roof, made up of centuries-old oak beams, until the spire collapsed onto part of the cathedral's vaulted transept. Firefighters rushed to try to save the rest of the building, which burned for almost fifteen hours. Addressing the shock and dismay of observers all over the world, President Macron observed that Notre-Dame was 'the cathedral of all the French people, even those who have never set foot in it'. The eventual rebuilding was a spectacular success – although there was criticism along the way of Macron's resistance to incorporating modifications into the work, as would typically have been done in the nineteenth century.

Paris, meanwhile, had again moved on politically. The city's mayor since 1995 had been Jean Tiberi, who was eventually convicted of vote-rigging. He was replaced in 2001 by the first of two socialists, Bertrand Delanoë, who was in turn succeeded in 2014 by his deputy, Spanish-born Anne Hidalgo. Delanoë benefited from a willingness to consider change, which helped him to appeal to a youngish constituency: he was responsible for the Paris-Plages (Paris-Beach) on the banks of the Seine each summer, and for making moves towards the restriction of road traffic. However, with congestion rising, the latter made road transport in the city much more difficult; furthermore, as many observed, it was one thing for Delanoë to talk of ending the 'museumification' of the city but quite another for him to actually deliver results.

Hidalgo continued Delanoë's efforts to limit car usage, as well as sharing his wider concern with environmentalism and the drive for cleaner air. In 2015, Paris was the setting for a major international climate conference that saw pledges to limit carbon emissions. The socialist mayor, who drew heavily on eastern Paris for support, also spoke of improving the relationship between east and west in the city by equalizing life chances. In 2020, she announced steps to halve the number of parking spaces in Paris and make it a so-called 15-minute city: one in which all the necessary amenities of life could be reached by a 15-minute walk or cycle ride. Mayor Hidalgo was unsuccessful as a candidate for the presidency in 2022, coming tenth. In part, this reflected Paris's general unpopularity within France, but there was also a crisis taking place within the Socialist Party.

The extent to which Paris is politically out of alignment with France as a whole has been a continuing issue in its politics. Typically the city has been more left-leaning than the Île-de-France

Renaming the city

IN JANUARY 2023 THE MAYOR OF PANTIN, A NORTH-EASTERN SUBURB first named in 1067 and now suffering from an air pollution problem, officially added an 'e' to its name for a period of twelve months – without consulting local residents. The idea behind this decision was to make it sound more feminine and thus, somehow, promote equality between the sexes.

and the rest of the country, but it also has internal divisions between areas that are predominantly left- or right-wing.

The Covid pandemic of 2020–22 hit Paris hard, not only in terms of the deaths incurred but also – as in major cities everywhere – by devastating its leisure and tourism sectors. Lockdowns in France were among the most restrictive anywhere in the world and the impact on the city's economy was profound, arguably greater than elsewhere in the country. Day-to-day life for Parisians was temporarily transformed: not only had all the tourists vanished but public transport was running at a minimal level, shops and offices were closed, and parks and green spaces locked up.

But if, for a time, Covid meant that the rest of the world could experience only a virtual Paris – a Paris at one remove, to be viewed online rather than appreciated in person – this would change in 2022, as the pandemic ended and travel to the city rapidly revived.

Chapter 15

Paris Today and in the Future

There is significant variation in character between the arrondissements of Paris. The last of these, the 20th, was characterized by the early twentieth-century essayist Léon-Paul Fargue as overlooked and lacking in facilities – without even sufficient electricity or transport at the time Fargue was writing, let alone anything to attract tourists – and yet people lived there and were busy and productive. Today, it is still well worth a visit for those interested in the Paris of residents. This Paris extends far beyond the area conventionally understood as 'the city' – a point that was emphasized in 2016 by the creation of a new administrative area known as Grand Paris (Greater Paris), bringing together 131 communes including the largest, Paris itself. To help unite this space, the Grand Paris Express transport scheme was constructed, including four new Métro lines as well as extensions to two others: a total of 200 kilometres, or 120 miles, of new track.

Grand Paris includes Sarcelles, a relatively new suburb that inspired the 1960s coinage 'Sarcellitis': a term for the misery and boredom of life in a soulless environment without human scale. It may have been used too loosely, given the miserable nature of earlier housing inadequacies, but it did capture a particular aspect of the contrasts within modern Paris. So too did the difference between a *banlieue aisée* – a 'comfortable suburb' like Sceaux – and one that was *défavorisée* or disadvantaged, such as Malakoff.

Cultural politics aside, Paris today has many difficulties: crime, dirty streets, homelessness, ethnic and racial tensions, overcrowded Métro trains, heavy-handed policing, traffic jams. All of these are issues most large cities face, with Paris offering both the same and yet much more in terms of its own particular response. In March 2023, a revival of the revolutionary tradition occurred in the form of strikes protesting an increase in the pension age for workers. The strikers included rubbish collectors (whose pension age was set to increase from 57 to 59) and by 13 March more than 5,000 tonnes of refuse were littering the pavements, encouraging the city's estimated 6.5 million rats. The heaps of rubbish marred famous silhouettes such as that of the Eiffel Tower on the esplanade of the Trocadéro.

The strike divided politicians, with Parisian mayor Anne Hidalgo speaking up in support while the mayors of the conservative arrondissements called for the use of private contractors to clean up the streets. Clashes between police and those supporting the strike became so intense that by 19 March there were water cannon on the Place de la Concorde, where protests had been banned, and near the Place d'Italie there were barricades made from burning rubbish and abandoned rental bicycles. The air smelt of tear gas. The following day, the *Financial Times* quoted an unnamed Parisian: 'It's war in the 13th arrondissement tonight, because otherwise we will all be working until we're 88.'

Despite the international headlines generated by this type of unrest, not to mention the city's many other challenges, the post-Covid years have seen tourists flocking back to Paris in significant numbers. By the summer of 2023, some of France's most popular sites were becoming so crowded that a government campaign against 'overtourism' was launched, encouraging people to consider a wider range of French holiday destinations for the sake of both the environment and residents' quality of life. Even so, Paris alone was projected to see more than 37 million visitors over the course of the year, most of them American or British.

For many tourists drawn to Paris by the 2024 Olympics (see plate XIX), the typical round of museums and historic sites may be less of a priority; instead, their principal impressions are likely to be of Charles de Gaulle Airport and the Stade de France. The Stade was inaugurated in 1998, when France not only hosted the World Cup but won it for the first time. Located in Saint-Denis, it is an impressive structure, elliptical in shape with a seating capacity of 80,698. It is widely regarded as one of the best stadiums in Europe. During a friendly match between France and Germany in November 2015, it was targeted in a terrorist attack by Islamic extremists – the effective security precautions worked well, and have been further enhanced in recent years.

Charles de Gaulle Airport dates from an earlier phase of twentieth-century development, having opened in 1974. As of 2019, it was Europe's busiest for passengers after Heathrow and the busiest overall for freight. It has three terminals, the first of which is a dramatic circular building; plans for a large new fourth terminal were derailed by the pandemic. The airport is linked to central Paris by slow RER services that take passengers through some unexpected parts of the city, but at the time of writing there are plans in place for an express, non-stop rail service to the Gare de l'Est.

Meanwhile, a major renovation of the Gare du Nord that was originally intended to take place in time for the 2023 Rugby World Cup had to be abandoned in 2021 after estimated costs rose sharply. A more modest renovation of the station, which remains notorious as a haunt of pickpockets and muggers, was launched instead.

OLYMPIC
COMPETITION VENUES MASTER PLAN

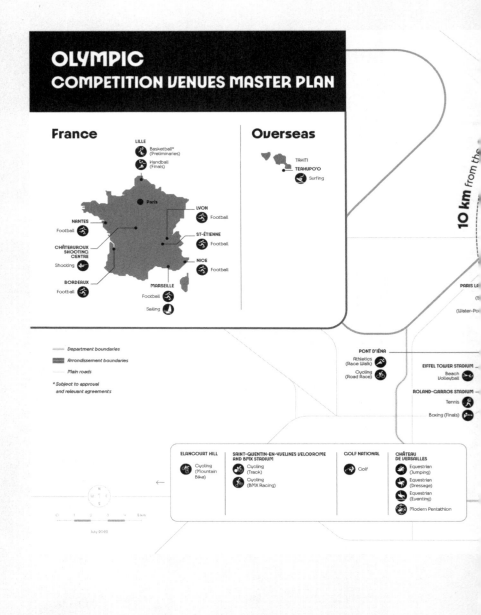

France

LILLE
Basketball* (Preliminaries)
Handball (Finals)

Paris

NANTES
Football

CHÂTEAUROUX SHOOTING CENTRE
Shooting

BORDEAUX
Football

LYON
Football

ST-ÉTIENNE
Football

NICE
Football

MARSEILLE
Football
Sailing

Overseas

TAHITI
TEAHUPO'O
Surfing

Department boundaries
Arrondissement boundaries
Main roads
* Subject to approval and relevant agreements

---

10 km from the

PARIS LA
(S
(Water-Po

PONT D'IÉNA
Athletics (Race Walk)
Cycling (Road Race)

EIFFEL TOWER STADIUM
Beach Volleyball

ROLAND-GARROS STADIUM
Tennis
Boxing (Finals)

ELANCOURT HILL
Cycling (Mountain Bike)

SAINT-QUENTIN-EN-YVELINES VELODROME AND BMX STADIUM
Cycling (Track)
Cycling (BMX Racing)

GOLF NATIONAL
Golf

CHÂTEAU DE VERSAILLES
Equestrian (Jumping)
Equestrian (Dressage)
Equestrian (Eventing)
Modern Pentathlon

0   1   2   3   4   5 km

July 2022

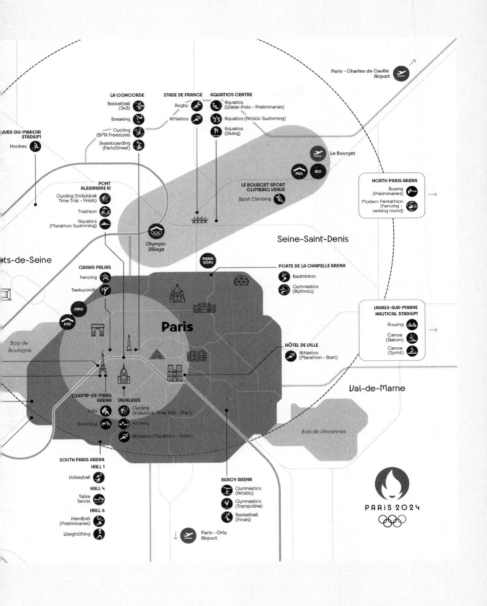

PSG

PARIS SAINT-GERMAIN FOOTBALL CLUB IS BASED IN THE PARC
des Princes. Known as the Parisians or the Red and Blues, the
club was founded in 1970 as the result of a merger between
Paris FC and the Stade Saint-Germain. The team has had a
rollercoaster ride, being hit by failure and serious debt in the late
1980s, but in 1991 it was taken over by the television company
Canal+ and refinanced, after which it went on to repeated
success in the 1990s.

In 2011 the club was purchased by Qatar Sports Investments
and became one of the wealthiest teams in the world. It is
important to the identity and fame of the city, although
this point is not always fully appreciated by followers of
the game.

Of course, travelling to Paris is not possible for everyone.
But today more than ever, in the age of streaming, the city has
a place in the imaginations of countless people who will never
see it in person. Far more viewers around the world now experience Paris through their television or tablet screens than by gazing
at paintings or prints. French film is internationally appreciated
and modern audiences can explore anything from the New
Wave classics of the 1950s and '60s, such as Jean-Luc Godard's
À bout de souffle (Breathless, 1960) or Jacques Rivette's *Paris
nous appartient* (Paris Belongs to Us, 1961), to acclaimed later
works like François Truffaut's *Le Dernier Métro* (The Last
Metro, 1980) or Leos Carax's *Les Amants du Pont-Neuf* (1991).
Over the years Paris has also been a popular setting for crime
dramas such as *Le Cercle Rouge* (The Red Circle, 1970) or the

hard-edged *La Haine* (Hate, 1995), which links urban rioting in a Paris banlieu to immigrant life, social division, violence and police brutality. In a completely different vein there is Jean-Pierre Jeunet's *Amélie* (2001), a fanciful Montmartre-set comedy that was a smash hit around the world.

Non-French films set in the city include Bernardo Bertolucci's *Last Tango in Paris* (1972) – still notorious fifty years on for its themes of anonymous sexual passion and violence – and Richard Linklater's acclaimed romance *Before Sunset* (2004). Blake Edwards' iconic comedy *The Pink Panther* (1963) takes place partly in Paris and features a glimpse of the Pont Saint-Louis before its rebuilding later that decade. Other classic American filmic homages include *Funny Face* (1957), *Paris When It Sizzles* (1964) and *How to Steal a Million* (1966); and then there is Disney/Pixar's *Ratatouille* (2007), a triumph of animation that emphasizes the city's historic charm with food and scenery to the fore.

A more recent (if not necessarily more realistic) popular depiction of Paris can be found in Netflix's wildly successful series *Emily in Paris* (2020–), starring Lily Collins as an expat American marketing manager living in the 5th arrondissement. It is a lightweight fantasy portrait of the city, but in an example of how hotly contested Paris's public image can be, there have been scathing attacks on the programme by French politicians. Early in 2023, David Belliard, the leader of the Paris Greens in charge of the city's transport and public spaces, wrote in *Libération*:

> It is a snapshot of an unchangeable Paris, a Disneyland, which is confined to the ultra-centre, inhabited only by the richest people in a uniform architectural heritage....The fable is neither desirable nor viable.

More generally, Belliard was angry about opposition in Paris to policies including the addition of cycle lanes and the removal of trees in order to install new tramlines: 'We have to get out of nostalgia for a stereotypical city.' Elsewhere, he has drawn attention to the difficult, even harmful environmental and residential consequences of traditional city centre housing. On the other hand, there has been much criticism of the pace of change demanded by a council that has pledged to transform the city environment and been critical of decisions made in the past. This process repeats various past episodes of self-styled reform.

Moreover, some aspects of the present city council's reform policy clash with other interests in Paris, often over what has been characterized as the deterioration of the city. The council has been vocal about the need to curb rentals on the Airbnb platform, which, it claims, are hollowing out historic districts and depriving residents of homes. In 2021 the council fined Airbnb eight million euros for advertising properties not registered with the council; it has also restricted rentals to owners' primary residences, and then for no more than four months each year. Money is at stake in these discussions: in 2022, 24.3 million euros in accommodation taxes were paid to the city from Airbnb rentals.

The modern approach to the conservation of built heritage ensures that even as many aspects of Parisian life change, historically significant buildings are protected. In the 1970s, when Les Halles was demolished, there was talk of demolishing the Gare d'Orsay too – but instead, following what has become a common pattern, it became a museum. Ironically, in this respect modern thinking is out of step with the past: demolition for the sake of 'progress' and development, whether in the wake of conflict or for purely political reasons, has been commonplace throughout much of history.

While the buildings of central Paris are well guarded nowadays, changes in the way they are used continue to be frequent, often as part of the embourgeoisement of areas that were previously working class. In the 1960s and '70s, 'urban renewal' meant the destruction not only of Les Halles – a city within a city and working-class enclave, with its distinctive nineteenth-century covered market halls built of iron and glass – but of numerous streets in other low-income areas, notably Belleville. In their place came endless high-rise flats, particularly in southern Paris. Also in the south of the city, but built for business, is the ugly, monolithic Tour Montparnasse, which was constructed in 1969–73 on the site of old housing and an old railway station; it was the tallest skyscraper in France until 2011, when the Tour First in La Défense had its height increased. The latter, also a 1970s structure, fits far better into its urban environment, both locally and more widely. Unlike London and New York, Paris has sought (if a little inconsistently, owing to occasional changes in planning laws) to maintain a limit on the height of buildings in the city centre, creating a classical skyline that most cities cannot match.

The future of Paris will probably align in some ways with that of other western European cities: it will continue to grow as a result of immigration, some of it illegal, while the non-immigrant population ages. Demographics are destiny, and Paris is no exception. Compared to much of Europe, France has relatively high population growth, but for the non-immigrant population this is presently strongest in rural areas where housing is cheaper. Some northern French cities, particularly those with a tradition of heavy industry such as Reims and Roubaix, have seen a fall in numbers in line with economic difficulties; meanwhile, there has been growth in some southern cities, notably Toulouse.

The demographic difficulties specific to much of northern France tend not to apply in Paris and its immediate surroundings, but the high cost of city life is certainly a factor, and especially so for families. In 2021 the average monthly rent for an apartment rose to 39 euros per square metre in the 1st arrondissement, and fell only to 29 euros in the 12th, 19th and 20th. Rents in some areas approached London figures. It can be difficult to find reliable population data for the city, but after a period of growth from 1997 (2.11 million) to early 2012 (2.24 million), there appears to have been a fall back to 2.14 million in early 2022. In short, recent decades have seen a degree of ebb and flow around a constant trend: a decline in the percentage of the French who live in Paris. Despite this, population density is certainly high, at 20,623 people per square kilometre as of 2021, and it is difficult to see how existing housing could readily take higher densities. There are brownfield sites, mostly railway and defence land, but it is unlikely much of this will be released for housing, not least because of the city's commitment to developing its public transport system.

By contrast, the wider area – Grand Paris – has a different population trajectory, one of significant growth. Its population in 2018 was 7.1 million. As Napoleon III demonstrated, the boundaries of Paris can be altered, and the 2016 reconceptualization of Grand Paris incorporated important sections of the Île-de-France: the departments of Hauts-de-Seine, Seine-Saint-Denis and Val-de-Marne were included, as were parts of Val-d'Oise and Essonne. This represented a total increase of 814 square kilometres (314 square miles), and as of 2018 the population density was 8,690 per square kilometre.

The typical tourist's assessment of Paris is likely to continue to be dominated by the city proper and within that, primarily its central areas; furthermore, the perception of this version of Paris in the popular imagination tends to be fairly traditional. Thus, what Paris *means* to visitors may, in the years to come, alter less than it should. Residents, though, are always aware of change – their understanding of the city in its larger sense, of its wider surroundings, shapes their day-to-day experience of living there. This was as true in the past as it is today; thus, in 1832, Chateaubriand observed of the cholera that had recently hit Paris, taking more than 18,000 lives: 'If this scourge had fallen upon us in a religious age…the wrath and judgement of God…the sacred relics [of Saint Geneviève would have been] carried round the city….[Instead] the cholera has come to us in an age of philanthropy, incredulity, newspapers, and material administration….This unimaginative scourge found no cloisters awaiting it, no monks, no vaults, no Gothic tombs…'

In 1883, two paintings by Pierre-Auguste Renoir were exhibited as a pair: *Danse à la ville* and *Danse à la campagne*, both now displayed in the Musée d'Orsay. There is a clear difference in mood between the formality of the former and the free form of the latter, reflecting a social contrast that is further emphasized in another Renoir of the same period, *Danse à Bougival* (Bougival, a suburb of Paris, was popular with the impressionists). The rural scenes convey impulse and joy, possibly passion; the city scene suggests elegance, chic and an artificiality of manner.

A sense of Paris often emerges this way, through contrast. No single image, of course, can capture it, as there is no single Paris. This is a city rich in the varied breaths of life; and that rich variety contributes much to the experience of visiting it, amply repaying the traveller.

BIBLIOGRAPHY

The majority of this bibliography refers to the books, plays and quotes that are directly referenced within each chapter. Therefore, a number of chapters are without citations. For a broader introduction to Paris's rich history please consult the titles below.

Druon, M., *The History of Paris: From Caesar to Saint Louis* (New York, 1969).
Higonnet, P., *Paris: Capital of the World* (Cambridge, MA, 2002).
Jenkins, C., *A Brief History of Paris* (Boston, MA, 2022).
Jones, C., *Paris: Biography of a City* (London, 2004).

Introduction
The Inevitability of Paris (pp. 6–11)
Colette, *'Gigi'* and *'The Cat'*, translated by R. Senhouse (London, 2001).
Stendhal, *Scarlet and Black*, translated by M. R. B. Shaw (Harmondsworth, 1953).
Zola, É., *La Bête humaine*, translated by L. Tancock (Harmondsworth, 1977).

Chapter 4
The Sixteenth Century (pp. 46–54)
Marlowe, C., *The Massacre at Paris* (1593), Project Gutenberg edition, https://www.gutenberg.org/files/1496/1496-h/1496-h.htm.
Rabelais, F., *The Terrible Deeds and Acts of Prowess of Pantagruel, King of the Dipsodes*, translated by Thomas Urquhart and Peter Antony Motteux (Paris, 1532).

Chapter 5
The Seventeenth Century (pp. 55–72)
Black, J., *The British and the Grand Tour* (London, 2011).
Black, J., *France: A Short History* (London, 2022).
Black, J., *Why Wars Happen* (London, 1998).
Cecil Papers, Hatfield House, Hatfield.
Douce Manuscripts, Bodleian Library, Oxford.
Drake, W., letter to his father, 4 October 1768.

Papers of the Drake family of Amersham, 1621–1938, D-DR/8/2/2, Buckinghamshire CRO, Aylesbury.

Perceval, Sir J., letter to D. Dering, 11 May 1726. Egmont Papers, Add. MS 47031, f. 170, British Library, London.

Shaw, J., *Letters to a Nobleman from a Gentleman Travelling Thro' Holland, Flanders and France* (London, 1709).

Chapter 6
An Age of Opulence, 1700-1750 (pp. 73-98)

Alexander, R. C. (ed.), *The Diary of David Garrick: Being a Record of His Memorable Trip to Paris in 1751* (Oxford, 1928).

Black, J., *British Diplomats and Diplomacy, 1688–1800* (Liverpool, 2001).

Black, J., *Eighteenth-Century Europe*, 2nd ed. (London, 1999).

Black, J., *France and the Grand Tour* (London, 2003).

Brogden, J., copybook of letters by James Brogden. Add. MS 57304, ff. 82, 84, 85, 90, British Library, London.

Daily Advertiser (London,) 27 January 1737.

Dawson Greene collection, DDGr F/3, f. 35, Lancashire CRO, Preston.

Douce Manuscripts 67, 46, Bodleian Library, Oxford.

Drake, W., letter to his father, 4 October 1768. Papers of the Drake family of Amersham, 1621–1938, D/DR/8/2/2, Buckinghamshire CRO, Aylesbury.

Fox, R., and A. Turner (eds), *Luxury Trades and Consumerism in Ancien Régime Paris* (Aldershot, 1998).

Francis Papers, Add. MS 40759, f. 20, British Library, London.

Hanbury-Williams Papers, vol. 75, fol. 19, Lewis Walpole Library, Farmington, CT.

Harcourt, G., Lord Nuneham, letter to Lady Elizabeth Harcourt, 1755. Hardwicke Papers, Add. MS 36249, f. 132, British Library, London.

Loudoun Papers, no. 11333, Huntington Library, San Marino, CA.

Macdonald, A., letter to W. Eden, n.d. Auckland Papers, Add. MS 34412, ff. 84–5, British Library, London.

Mellish, E., letter to his father, 25 April 1731. Mellish Collection, MeC 24/3, Nottingham University Library, Nottingham.

Mildmay Family Archives, D/DM O1, Essex CRO, Chelmsford.

Millard, J., *Gentleman's Guide in his Tour through France. By an Officer who lately travelled on a principle which he most sincerely recommends to his countrymen, viz., not to spend more money in the country of our national enemy than is required to support with decency the character of an Englishman*, 7th ed. (London, 1783).

Mitford, J., travel journals, 1776–1791. Mitford Papers, D2002/3/4/1, 94, Gloucestershire Archives, Gloucester.

Ms. Eng. Misc. d. 213, 163–4. Bodleian Library, Oxford.

Osborn File, 19.252, Beinecke Rare Book and Manuscript Library, Yale University, New Haven, CT.

Perceval, Sir J., letter to Edward Southwell, 7 May 1726. Egmont Papers, Add. MS 47031, f. 169, British Library, London.

Reichel, Rev. O. J. (ed.), 'Extracts from a Devonshire lady's travel in France in the eighteenth century [Jane Parminter, 1750–1810, of A la Ronde, Exmouth]', *Transactions of the Devonshire Association for the Advancement of Science, Literature and Art* 34 (1902): 265–75.

Seymour, G., Lord Beauchamp, letter to Lord Hertford, 12 November 1742. Letters, vol. 113, Northumberland Papers, Alnwick Castle, Alnwick.

Sir Jolin Jervis Correspondence, Add. MS 31192, f. 12, British Library, London.

Supplementary Mitchell Papers, vol. XXXII, Add. MS 58314, ff. 8, 27. British Library, London.

Thicknesse, P., *Useful Hints to Those Who Make the Tour of France* (London, 1768).

Thomas, E., letter to Jeremiah Milles, 11 June 1750. Letters of Jeremiah Milles, Dean of Exeter, Add. MS 19941, f. 1, British Library, London.

Wharton, R., letter to Miss Lloyd, 29 February 1775. Wharton Papers 167, f. 2, Durham University Library, Durham.

Chapter 7
Towards Revolution, 1750–1789 (pp. 99–110)

Bennet, W., Continental travel diary. Ms. Eng. Misc. f. 54, ff. 174–5, Bodleian Library, Oxford.

Black, J., *France and the Grand Tour* (London, 2003).
Brand, T., letter to Robert Wharton, 10 May 1781. Wharton
    Papers 551, Durham University Library, Durham.
Crewe, F. A., *An English Lady in Paris: The Diary
    of Frances Anne Crewe, 1786* (Oxford, 2006).
Moore, J. C., *Life of Lieutenant General Sir John Moore* (n.p., 1833).
Wharton, R., letter to Thomas Brand, 17 March 1775.
    Wharton Papers 114, Durham University Library, Durham.
Windham Papers, Add. MS 37926, f. 70, British Library, London.

Chapter 8
Revolution and Napoleon, 1789-1815 (pp. 111-27)

Black, J., *British Foreign Policy in an Age of Revolutions,
    1783–1793* (Cambridge, 1994).
Black, J., *War in the Nineteenth Century, 1800–1914*
    (Cambridge, 2009).
Brillat-Savarin, J. A., *A Handbook of Gastronomy:
    Brillat-Savarin's Physiologie du goût* (London, 1884).
Buller, J., Buller journal, n.d. 2065 M/CI/1, f. 5. Devon
    CRO, Exeter.
Papers of Osborne, Francis Godolphin (1751–1799),
    5th Duke of Leeds, U269/C163-74, Kent History and
    Library Centre, Maidstone.
Sackville, John Frederick, 3rd Duke of Dorset, letter to
    Sir Nathaniel William Wraxall, 14 May 1789. Osborn MSS
    File 4529, Beinecke Rare Book and Manuscript Library,
    Yale University, New Haven, CT.
Stendhal, *Love*, translated by G. Sale and S. Sale
    (Harmondsworth, 2004).

Chapter 9
Restored Monarchy to War, 1815-1870 (pp. 128-46)

Balzac, H. de, *Lost Illusions* (*Illusions perdues*), translated
    by Herbert J. Hunt (Harmondsworth, 1971).
Dickens, C., *A Tale of Two Cities* (London, 1859).
Marx, K., *The Class Struggles in France, 1848 to 1850*,
    https://www.marxists.org/archive/marx/works/1850/
    class-struggles-france/ch01.htm.
Zola, É., *Nana*, translated by G. Holden
    (New York, 1972).

Chapter 10
Belle Époque, 1871–1914 (pp. 147–61)

Black, J., *Fortifications and Siegecraft: Defense and Attack Through the Ages* (Lanham, 2018).

King, R. J., 'Travellers and handbooks', *Edinburgh Review* 138 (1873): 483–510.

Marx, K., 'The third address (May, 1871)', https://www.marxists.org/archive/marx/works/1871/civil-war-france/ch06.htm.

Maupassant, G., *Bel-ami*, translated by D. Parmée (Harmondsworth, 1975).

Richardson, J. (ed.), *Paris under Siege* (London, 1980).

Stovall, T., *The Rise of the Paris Red Belt* (Berkeley, 2018).

Zola, É., *The Debacle*, translated by L. Tancock (London and New York, 1972).

Chapter 11
First World War and Interwar, 1914–1939 (pp. 162–76)

Carr, J. D., *It Walks by Night* (London, [1930] 2020).

Channon, H., *Henry 'Chips' Channon: The Diaries 1943–57*, edited by Simon Heffer (London, 2022).

Simenon, G., *Maigret et le corps sans tête* (Paris, 1955).

Simenon, G., *Pietr-le-Letton* (Paris, 1931).

Chapter 12
Second World War, 1939–1945 (pp. 177–85)

Hollande, F., '70th anniversary of the Vel d'Hiv roundup', speech given in Paris, 22 July 2012, *France in the US*, https://franceintheus.org/spip.php?article3784.

Jackson, J., *France on Trial: The Case of Marshal Pétain* (Penguin, 2023).

Chapter 13
Postwar Developments, 1945–1981 (pp. 186–96)

Fleming, I., 'From a View to a Kill', in *Five Secret Occasions in the Life of James Bond* (London, 1960).

'The history of Emmaus', *Emmaus*, https://emmaus.org.uk/hertfordshire/emmaus-history/.

Chapter 15
Paris Today and in the Future (pp. 206–217)

Bremner, C., '*Emily in Paris* ignores imperatives of climate change, says deputy mayor', *The Times*, 16 January 2023.

Chateaubriand, F., *Mémoires d'outre-tombe*, Book XXXIV, translated by R. Baldick (Penguin, 1972).

Klasa, A., and L. Abboud, 'Protests mount as Macron faces no-confidence vote on pensions reform', *Financial Times*, 19 March 2023.

ACKNOWLEDGMENTS

I am very grateful to Ben Hayes for asking me to write this book, to my late father for first taking me to the city, to a variety of grant-aiding bodies that have supported my work there since 1979, notably the archival collection in the National Archives, the National Library, the Army and Foreign Office archives, and those of the Arsenal Library, the Institute of France and the Sorbonne. I would like to thank the friends who have provided hospitality, particularly Matt Burrows, Michel Fleury, Hughes Mantoux, Bruno Neveu, Peter Sheldrick and Peter Tibber, and to those who commented on an earlier draft, notably Alan Forrest, Bill Gibson, Colin Jones and Frédéric Saffroy. They are not responsible for any errors or problems that remain. Ben Hayes has been a supportive editor and India Jackson a helpful desk editor.

Those visiting Paris who wish to take this further should look around them but in particular visit the museum of the history of Paris in the Hôtel Carnavalet in the Marais, as well as the nearby library of Paris in the Hôtel de Lamoignon, another original sixteenth-century building. A history of Paris is also a history of France, for the capital is so closely associated with this general history. To leave the latter out would be wrong.

It is a great pleasure to dedicate this book to Patrick Manning, a great and inspiring historian and a much valued friend.

ILLUSTRATION CREDITS

Sources of colour illustrations by plate number:

I Photo RMN-Grand Palais (musée de Cluny–musée national du Moyen Âge)/Jean-Gilles Berizzi/Gérard Blot; II Archives nationales, Paris; III Rostislav Glinsky/Alamy Stock Photo; IV Jan Willem van Hofwegen/Alamy Stock Photo; V Musée cantonal des Beaux-Arts de Lausanne; VI Photo RMN-Grand Palais (Château de Versailles)/ Gérard Blot; VII Only France/Alamy Stock Photo; VIII Photo RMN-Grand Palais (Château de Versailles)/Gérard Blot; IX Timken Collection, The National Gallery of Art, Washington, D.C.; X John Kellerman/Alamy Stock Photo; XI Musée de la Révolution française, Grenoble. Photo Christie's Images/Bridgeman Images; XII Musée d'Orsay, Paris; XIII Musée d'Orsay, Paris; XIV Philadelphia Museum of Art. Gift of Helen Tyson Madeira, 1991; XV Photo 12/Alamy Stock Photo; XVI Philippe Gras/Alamy Stock Photo; XVII Only France/ Alamy Stock Photo; XVIII Hemis/Alamy Stock Photo; XIX Reproduced by permission of The International Olympic Committee

Sources of black-and-white illustrations by page number:

2 Life on white/Alamy Stock Photo; 16–17 *Atlas General Histoire et Geographie*, Paul Vidal de La Blache, 1912; 24–5, 40–1 Bibliothèque nationale de France; 50–1 Universiteitsbibliotheek Vrije Universiteit, Amsterdam; 58–9 Bibliothèque nationale de France; 76–7 David Rumsey Map Collection, David Rumsey Map Center, Stanford Libraries; 102–3, 114–15 The Eran Laor Cartographic Collection, The National Library of Israel; 132–3 Published by Garnier Freres, 1864; 150–1 National Library of Sweden, The Royal Library; 166–7 Robelin Map of Paris, *c.* 1932; 180–1 Courtesy Tim Bryars. Photo Pariser Plan/British Library Board. All Rights Reserved/Bridgeman Images; 190–1 Ville de Paris/BHVP; 200–1 Designer Constantine Konovalov/metromap.fr; 210–11 Reproduced by permission of The International Olympic Committee

INDEX

Italic page numbers indicate illustrations.